MW01118098

Philadelphia Proverbs

Wisdom and Everyday Life

Brett L. Brooks

WESTBOW
PRESS®
A DIVISION OF THOMAS NELSON
& ZONDERVAN

Copyright © 2016 Brett L. Brooks.

All rights reserved. No part of this book may be used or reproduced by any means, graphic, electronic, or mechanical, including photocopying, recording, taping or by any information storage retrieval system without the written permission of the author except in the case of brief quotations embodied in critical articles and reviews.

Scripture taken from the King James Version of the Bible.

WestBow Press books may be ordered through booksellers or by contacting:

WestBow Press
A Division of Thomas Nelson & Zondervan
1663 Liberty Drive
Bloomington, IN 47403
www.westbowpress.com
1 (866) 928-1240

Because of the dynamic nature of the Internet, any web addresses or links contained in this book may have changed since publication and may no longer be valid. The views expressed in this work are solely those of the author and do not necessarily reflect the views of the publisher, and the publisher hereby disclaims any responsibility for them.

Any people depicted in stock imagery provided by Thinkstock are models, and such images are being used for illustrative purposes only. Certain stock imagery © Thinkstock.

ISBN: 978-1-5127-4165-0 (sc)
ISBN: 978-1-5127-4166-7 (hc)
ISBN: 978-1-5127-4164-3 (e)

Library of Congress Control Number: 2016907557

Print information available on the last page.

WestBow Press rev. date: 05/17/2016

Contents

Preface

Note the following passage. "Soap cleans the outside; repentance cleans the inside." An immediate question arises: What does it mean? It is basic human instinct to desire to understand the meaning of a thing. Without understanding there is no settlement in our thinking an uneasiness pervades, and there is a restlessness to know "What is its meaning?"

A "proverb" is defined as a brief saying giving advice on how a person should live or expressions of beliefs generally accepted to be true. *Philadelphia Proverbs* is a book that engages the reader to examine what is being said. The above saying, "Soap cleans the outside; repentance cleans the inside." is one of *Philadelphia Proverbs*'s many sayings. On average, a Christian understands repentance to be a reversal in one's conduct before God, but in this instance, liking it to "soap," identifies repentance to be also a cleansing agent. I knew that by repentance I walked away from sin. What I didn't know was that by walking away, I was also cleansed of my sin.

A proverb expands the meaning of a simply stated ideal whose truth is married to Scripture by lending itself to a broader interpretation of Scripture as it relates to everyday life.

In addition to its proverbs is its poetry. Common everyday themes dealing with everyday human experience are a featured portion of the book. By their cadence and beautifully articulated verse memorable poetic expression is shared with the reader.

Poetry is one of the world's most passionate forms of expression. A few words that speak volumes on any subject imaginable! Poetry, once written, is a shared experience. The writer pours out his or her soul's pain or personal joy and the reader is not only drawn through its passages as identifiable experience, but also benefits by its conclusions, which are lessons in life learned by another, the writer. Poetry is, therefore, another's journey which is shared by others.

Scriptural references appearing throughout the book have numbered endnote indicators. The corresponding endnotes at the end of the book display the referenced Scripture in full. This gives the reader the opportunity to compare *Philadelphia Proverbs* with biblical Scripture.

To my fellow Philadelphians … and the world

The spirit, the element …
My Spirit Is the Fire

My body is the element;
My spirit is the fire.
My soul's the member in between
That merges heart's desire.
Spirit coincides with mind,
The soul, imagination,
And body with the manifest
The end of God's creation.
Faith, substance, body are as one;
Imagination, hope, and soul;
Love, mind, and Spirit, unison
Can only wisdom's eye behold.
So my body's element combines
To be my spirit's fire,
And soul's imagination will
Take my being always higher.

1. Honey is sweet to the taste. Love is honey to the soul.

2. A man who seeks the approval of other men is limited by their opinions of him.

3. Before a thing is seen, faith is its only reality (Hebrews 11:1). [1]

4. Sadly, for many, life's mystery is unveiled to them only at life's end.

5. Outward beauty can deceive the beholder.

6. The eye that sees, sees only what it understands. The ear that hears, hears only what it believes.

7. Children left to wander through life on their own will wander into mischief.

8. Death and change are synonymous, and both equally feared.

9. The worst thing that can happen to you hasn't happened yet.

10. In a classroom if the student is not paying attention what good to him is the lesson?

Sometimes I wonder …
What Makes Flowers Grow?

What makes flowers grow?
What makes seasons last?
What makes strength appear in man?
What removes man from his past?
What makes time stand still?
What gives the sea its bounds?
What awesome thought created man
Or did with air the earth surround?
Who provided life a place to stay?
What makes hope appear?
What gives man a mind to pray?
What redemptive force relieves his fear?
What causes birds to sing?
What makes flowers grow?
Had I the answer to these things,
Then all secret things on earth I'd know.

11. Love will save the world.

12. With friendship there are no empty tomorrows.

13. Joy has a formula, just like God has a Son.

14. War has many casualties.

15. A man who loves money is easily corrupted by it (1 Timothy 6:10).[2]

16. Physical and mental discipline without moral discipline: Nothing from nothing leaves ...

17. War waged with the sword alone is rarely won by it.

18. Love is a little word with God behind it!

19. None of us really have any time left on this earth; we just keep borrowing it.

To melt icy mountains of indifference only takes ...

One Smile

One smile among the frozen faces,
one smile that seemed so obsolete.
One smile against the desert places
of drought and hunger, of love deplete.
One smile that brave and boldly challenged
the others who did coldly stare.
One smile through all did remain balanced,
and of its warmth did freely share.
One smile did as an island stand
against the selfish hearts of men.
One smile but led of love's command
did teach the world to smile again.

20. Giants are measured more in heart than in inches.

21. Choice is a powerful tool that some have used to become powerful people.

22. The solution to a problem found for one is the solution to a problem found for many.

23. Many people think that they learned how to add things up in the third grade, but they didn't.

24. Continuous pessimism may be an indication that one's enthusiasm has shorted out.

25. The person you are is not the one you see in the mirror.

26. The man who hates God does not understand who he really hates (Exodus 20:5).[3]

27. Wealth has to do with how much of the "inner kingdom" one has attained (Luke 17:20).[4]

28. Good ideas are little treasures that, if planted, grow into wealthy empires.

29. Sometimes the hardest part of getting well is just taking the medicine.

30. Many have failed. Some have gotten over it.

31. When you talk to God, it only seems like you are doing all the talking.

32. A man who does not love a woman from his heart, having partaken of her body, despises her (2 Samuel 13:14,15).[5]

33. Leaders ought also to be suggestion-oriented.

34. The unbelieving heart often claims that God has never said anything to it.

35. Things increase when you imagine they do (Hebrews 11:1).[6]

36. Though the apples in a master's painting appear very real, they cannot be tasted. The same holds true for religious pretense.

37. Giving is receiving in reverse.

38. The outpouring of God's wisdom is as when one taps, in season, into a maple tree.

39. Take heed to barking dogs.

40. Mankind is life discovering itself.

41. The motorist who drives too fast for conditions is asking calamity to be his road master.

42. Don't fight back with hate; fight back with love.

43. The saved are timeless.

44. No matter how big the house, you can still occupy only one room at a time. No matter how fancy the car, it can still only take you from one place to another. No matter how expensive the suit, its job is only to shelter you from the cold. And no matter how much you accumulate in this life, you still can't take any of it with you when you go (Job 1:21).[7]

45. As quickly as your face and name are out of the media mainstream people forget who you are.

46. To age in wisdom is to not grow old.

47. A seed never dies, but when planted in the earth and watered, springs out of its tiny tomb over and over again, from life to life (Psalm 90:2).[8]

48. Men daily dream of attaining powers they already possess (Luke 17:20–21).[9]

49. When a man casts a baited hook attached to the strong line of his hope into the turbulent waters of his desire, he does not always "catch" what he was looking for.

50. Individuals bored with their own lives usually find interest in other people's business.

51. Without pain, the body would not know that it was in danger of dying. The same holds true in life in regard to one's soul.

52. If men stopped dreaming, the world would still be there, but new worlds would never appear!

53. The man's road, who feels he can go nowhere in life, is crossed by mental barricades.

54. Love is more important than things.

55. The orange drinks the sunshine. Man drinks the orange(juice); therefore, man drinks the sunshine.

56. If you live in the past, you die in the past.

57. Have you found what you're looking for yet?

58.   The first step is asking. The next step is affirming.

59.   Small children left unattended for any length of time could very easily end up dead.

The mystical moment of a day's beginning …

At Dawn

The peak of dawn, whilst the world still sleeps,
I go to my window and take a peak …
Awesome moment of stillness like magic portrayed;
I soak in its splendor, and time is delayed.
Neither darkness nor light, but somewhere between,
Such as this, godly wonder, by my eyes are now seen.
The magic is haunting; the world is a hush.
The things I am feeling, to speak of's too much.
Break of day is a silence bespeaking the dawn.
In my heart silence utters, "All your troubles are gone!"
And I wrinkle my brow as I wonder, *How so?*
Again from the silence, "Be still, oh man know!"
So at dawn's first of morning most the world's still asleep.
As I stayed at my window, godly silence did speak:
"I am with you, my child, at this peak of the dawn,
And I still will be with you when the shadows are drawn;
I'll be there forever, let your hope not grow dim,
For the calm of day's dawning lies forever within."

60.   When the mind and the heart work together, mysteries are unraveled!

61.   If Jesus is meek and lowly, what ought a Christian to be (Matthew 11:29)?[10]

62.   The soul destitute of wisdom is easily attracted to that which is not knowledge (Proverbs 7:5–7).[11]

63. Jesus died for you. Are you willing to *die* for Jesus?

64. Good is all around you. Just think what it would be like to have it in you!

65. To teach a child to kill, don't teach him not to (Exodus 20:13).[12]

66. All living things on earth bring forth after their kind. Which living thing do you think thought that up (Genesis 1:21)?[13]

67. God placed man on earth to dress and keep his garden (Genesis 2:15).[14]

68. God crowns each new day with morning!

69. If you haven't made your peace with God, your heart is liable to be "attacked" at any time.

70. When a leader is *sent,* it is with an unstoppable purpose!

71. Seeds are thoughts. Thoughts are seeds.

72. The man who desires to better himself keeps his mind on things above (Colossians 3:2).[15]

73. Blessing after blessing follows the righteous.

74. Even the ocean, unreplenished, will eventually evaporate.

75. That which is alluring to the flesh is quicksand.

I have …
A Dream

A dream is something awesome.
A dream is something free;
My dream is something that I know
By faith, someday I'll see.
A dream perceives tomorrow
As not different from today;
It says to "wait on me, my child,

I'll bring your hope without delay."
A dream, if held within you
Will come true every time,
For substance is built on things not seen
(Hebrews 11:1).[16]
Reality's but a phase of dream's design.

76. It is not a crime to not have anything because you can always get. It is, however, a sin to not want anything because then you can never have anything.

77. Do you really think one's soul dies?

78. The son who is allowed to be instructed by his peers will one day be visited in prison.

79. Prays. Praise. Prays. Praise.

80. People are not as different from one another as they think they are.

81. The heart is the whole man.

82. God is "same-day-service."

83. Sin's connection to man, is man's connection to sin.

84. Truly great men rarely consider themselves to be so.

85. Some glances cut just like knives do.

86. Get it done now.

It cannot see …
Love Is Blind

Love is blind; its eyes don't see
Your shortcomings, your negativity.
Love is whole, complete, and sound,

Though slighted it will still be found …
Ever by your side, in fact,
Its loving nature remains intact.
For love is blind and will remain,
Though its little life be filled with pain.
Love is blind. Love is blind.

87. Segregation is one of the parents of cruelty.

88. The juvenile delinquent is a product of child neglect.

89. Some philosophers refer to a man overcoming his circumstances as "The triumph of the human spirit." Properly stated, the phrase would read, "The triumph of the Spirit of God in the human."

90. Fear forever resides in the house of a sinful soul.

91. Worldliness is the discipline of the undisciplined.

92. The man closest to the ground is the easiest to step on.

93. Everything you do is preempted by choice.

94. The mighty lion in a cage of steel bars remains there. So, too, does a man set in his ways.

95. Whatever you want to be, think it.

96. No matter what the time of day or weather conditions, the sun is always shining … somewhere.

97. Though unwilling to admit the fact that it does, unrepentant man's greatest fear awaits him.

98. True independence is realized when one understands he or she is totally dependent on God (John 5:19).[17]

99. Elected officials only sometimes serve the public will.

100. Change sometimes has to do with nickels, dimes, quarters, and pennies … Change sometimes has to do with making change(es).

101. Only when experience is drawn upon is it valuable.

102. Fear and faith do not coexist: Where you find faith you do not find fear. Where you find fear you cannot find faith (1 John 4:18).[18]

103. The smaller matter gets (e.g., as in the examination of protons, neutrons, and electrons), the more theory there is involved in the explanation of its very existence as substance (quantum physics) (Hebrews 11:1).[19]

104. When a man can ignore the fact that there are obstacles before him, they become instantly immaterial.

105. Giving someone something for nothing is not the same as giving someone something for Christmas.

106. Marital infidelity is a part-time involvement with full-time consequences.

107. The sun may one day not rise, but God will always still be God.

108. A smile, though a physical action, somehow spreads emotional sunshine throughout one's entire being.

109. With this new breed of mothers who wait on their children hand and foot and refuse to teach them responsibility, their children really have it "maid."

110. If a man does not believe in what he cannot see, then what is an idea?

111. The tongue of the serpent is wise but not loving.

112. Your opponent …? yourself.

113. Physical attraction, over time, rarely translates into emotional harmony.

They take only from themselves when …
They Steal Their Chances to Be Free

They slip into the evening places,
Into the crawl spaces of night …
They disappear into the darkness shadows,

Thinking their deeds are out of sight.
They steal from one another their chances to be free;
They eat the bread they think so sweet when eaten secretly.
They do forsake the sacred and immerse in the unclean;
They combine unholy mingle that forges consequence unseen.
They think not that a marriage may be union from above;
She betrays her husband, while her suitor steals his love.
But they steal from one another their chances to be free,
They destroy their souls through wickedness
By what they think's done secretly.

114. Leadership threads the needle that attaches, as one, the quilt of humanity!

115. Sin is a continually beguiling snake, seeking always entrance into the garden of one's paradise.

116. The heart is an unsearchable sea (Jeremiah 17:9).[20]

117. You can't fight love because love won't fight you back.

118. A safe may be strong, but it is still not always *safe* to keep (all) your money there.

119. The "church" is a place built in one's heart that stands upon the foundation of one's faith (Matthew 16:18).[21]

Though I had not much to offer …
I Fed the Hungry for a Day

I fed the hungry for a day and did a sincere love portray.
I gave them meat and bread and such;
through food I taught them God's love much.
Can I enjoy a well-cooked meal
with my neighbor starved and chilled and ill?

To impart the godly master plan,
God needs hearts and bread-filled hands.
And why do you, my friend, stand by
while with hunger the children cry?
We need a portion of your pay to feed the hungry for a day.

Can I partake of a goodly pot
while my neighbor partakes of it not?
And satisfy my appetite
while many a soul goes to bed hungry at night?
I ask you please, again I say,
would you feed the hungry for a day?

Some eat out of garbage cans,
their silent cries make no demands.
Their tears are sheltered far from view,
but their cries echo deep inside of you.
It's time to get busy, and make no delay,
to feed the hungry for a day.

Clothe and shelter, show kindness, too,
as godly love has oft showed you.
Seek those in need, extend your hand,
help heal, uplift your fellow man!
It's not so hard, I hope, I pray, to feed the hungry for a day.

And you'll be blessed; I won't deny
that you've dried the tears from some tear-filled eyes,
and you've filled with bread some hungry soul
From your heart within that once waxed cold.
And you followed Jesus and his blessed way,
and you fed the hungry for a day!

120. Satan knows that God did not create an unintelligent man, therefore, he mixes truth with his lies (Genesis 3:1).[22]

121. When anyone has the ability to choose his or her own thoughts, and we all do, why not take advantage of that opportunity and choose only good ones (Philippians 4:8)?[23]

122. Warning: it's coming (back) around (Galatians 6:7)![24]

123. Thoughts touch things.

124. The more one yields of himself to God, the more of life's mysteries, unraveled, God yields to him.

125. Conserve energy. Stop worrying.

126. Lust, by its very nature, can never be satisfied.

127. When David faced Goliath, there was no fear in his slingshot (1 Samuel 17:32).[25]

128. Tell the world that Jesus saves, and it will laugh. At a future date— and time—get yourself a visitor's pass, attend hell briefly, and remind them of how funny it was.

129. Little dreams, little futures.

130. A necessary project left incomplete stalls human progress.

131. Men are stoppable; ideas are not!

132. Every man God took the time to create is of immeasurable worth. The man who wastes what God took the time to create is immeasurably worthless (Matthew 25:24–30).[26]

133. Want to work hard and suffer for the rest of your life? Don't discipline your children.

134. Give equal time to your imagination.

135. If Pontius Pilate found no fault in Jesus, why then did he scourge him (John 19:1)?[27]

136. Once a prisoner of Jesus Christ, you receive a *life sentence* (Ephesians 3:1).[28]

137. Dreams are mirrored and reflected messages from God's mysterious deep (Job 33:14–16).[29]

138. "He that receiveth you receiveth me, and he that receiveth me receiveth him that sent me." Simple math (Matthew 10:40).[30]

139. Satan urges us to do very foolish things like take the name of the Lord our God in vain (Exodus 20:7).[31]

140. Justice may not always be swift, but it is very, very sure.

Most do not appreciate …
A Dollar's Value

A dollar's value, one drop in bucket,
Mounting one by one to top.
And soon your bucket's full of dollars
That started from one single drop.

141. Since people who gamble say that they do it because it's fun. Why then are their faces so long after they finish losing several hundred (or several thousand) dollars at the casino?

142. The body is made of what goes into it; the heart by what comes out of it (Matthew 15:11).[32]

143. It is mostly what a someone is not that he or she ends up trying to defend.

144. They say "safe sex." What they didn't tell you is that there's nothing safe about fornication (Romans 1:29).[33]

145. Satan disguises himself in the costume of desire.

146. That which I borrowed from my neighbor but never gave back I stole from my neighbor (Psalm 37:21).[34]

147. Once planted in the mind, a thought increases in size and becomes set in direction.

148. Faith replaces doubt; that is, if you have the faith to let it (Mark 9:24).[35]

149. The best things in life are virtually unknown to man(Isaiah 64:4; 1 Corinthians 2:9).[36]

150. To be *you* is a gift.

151. What goes on in your head will end up in your heart.

152. Everything Satan has something to do with turns out just like him ... ugly (Matthew 13:27, 28).[37]

153. Nothing alive breathes on its own (Genesis 2:7).[38]

154. You never know how small your world is until you wander into bigger ones.

155. The first step is to admit where you are, and from there you can move forward.

156. There is a balance between saving and spending; he who finds it is not called a penny pincher, he is called a businessman.

157. Where this world limits you, the world of dreams invites you.

158. What is real? What is imagined? And what, if any, is the difference between the two?

159. One's hunger in the soul will never be satisfied by bread alone (Luke 4:4).[39]

160. An individual who searches for answers will soon find them (Matthew 7:7).[40]

161. Do you feel pretty on the inside? If you don't, you should.

162. A created being, being created, creates (Genesis 1:26, 27).[41]

163. Lucifer exalted himself to heights he could never attain (Isaiah 14:12–15).[42]

164. Long life is called eternal life.

165. The person who finds, feels with their heart. The person who feels with their heart, finds with their soul. The person whose soul feels what it finds, finds God and is filled with what they feel in their soul.

It winds; it turns into a most desired end …

Promise Bend

Winding, turning promise bend, my heart yearns ere to see,
Desires fan a flaming hope for things I wish could be.
Winding turns, uncertainty, when fiendish doubt appears,
Its aim to stifle freedom and to make hope disappear.
But I do travel promise bend where hope does always live,
And I will realize my dreams when my fears to God I give,
For he alone is promise bend, and on his Word I stand,
I do not fear world's treachery, obeying his commands.
God's promise: To fulfill all dreams and life for evermore (Psalm 21:2),[43]
So travel promise bend with me, and we'll walk through heaven's door.

166. What people have to say about you, especially when it is negative, is generally what they *know* of themselves to be true.

167. As the determined path of a destructive storm cannot be turned, no one on earth can stem the tide of public opinion.

168. All words have meaning. So what do you mean when you use the wrong words?

169. To understand the world around you, just look at the big picture (Matthew 24:7).[44]

170. Where money is being made honestly, let not the wealth be spread disproportionately.

171. If a parent preaches one thing and does another, the children they raise will grow up to preach one thing and do another.

172. There is a way that seemeth right to a man, but it is not at all what it seemeth (Proverbs 14:12).[45]

173. Men's hearts are rich in ungodliness.

174. Stress is simply the mental overmanagement of one's problems. Relief from stress is the relinquishing of one's overmanagement to the head of stress management … God.

175. A woman who reveals more of herself in public than is mete (as in mode of dress), calls attention to herself for reasons other than making a fashion statement.

The fall is here and now …
The Summer Is Gone

The summer is gone with all that it meant,
The things that we shared, the times that we spent.
That warmth, once enjoyed, has faded away,
Has gone its far journey; no more exists as today.
From it we have salvaged the things that might last,
The things not absorbed or swept away with the past:
Inspiration and love, friendship and faith,
The good we aspired with every falsehood erased.
Times that may linger we hold in our hearts;
Life's lasting riches that will never depart.
Yes, it is gone, but not the meaning it gave,
For the things in our hearts in our hearts will be saved.
The summer is gone, but with its passing is spared
All the treasured belongings for which we have cared.

176. Just because God gives you some things does not mean that you are in a position for him to give you all things.

177. People don't ask questions about things they don't want to know the answers to.

178. I'm not much on color differences, but I am big on people similarities.

179. How can anyone stop that which is meant to be?

180. The so-called intangible things like love, trust, honesty, patience, and the like will produce in your life only intangible things like peace, joy, happiness, satisfaction, and the like.

181. A man's eyes can never see truth his heart refuses to.

182. Desire left unchecked is like a tiny smoldering ash in a dry wood that eventually sets the entire soul on fire.

183. Children left to their own thoughts will be filled with thoughts not their own.

184. The proper translation for the word "ignor"-ance is "I don't want to know!"

185. Youth is not a physical thing; it's a mind thing.

186. The ungodly act that you commit now may seem sweet and to your liking, but the aftertaste is murder.

Too many …
Misunderstandings

Misunderstandings tear lives apart;
They cause mankind to suffer so.
They take the heart's so loving nature,
There, sowing tares that grow and grow.
Misunderstandings break love's stride,
Chilling hearts to standing still,
For true love is now oft denied,

Embittered by a poisoned will.
Misunderstandings oft interpret
Things in awkward ways unjust,
Refusing needful audience
So that the matter be discussed.
Misunderstandings snap the heartstrings
That bind true love to soul and will.
Misunderstandings are of life's sad things,
Tis happy union's bitter pill.

187. In a monogamist society, a woman who is willing to "share" a so-called man with another woman is only half a woman.

188. Children, like sponges, absorb the world around them.

189. Replace a thought with a thought.

190. Your number may be up … next (Luke 12:16-20).[46]

191. A man oft provoked to anger is easily led to his own destruction (Psalm 37:8).[47]

192. A tree that fails to bud in the spring is dead. So, too, is the man with no new ideas.

193. Give into your child where discipline is sorely needed, and you will always gain that child's disrespect.

I saw a delightful …
Window Dressed

Window dressed in Christmas lights.
Such friendly sights, the lights.
Snapping briskly, they wink at me;
Smiling, alarming, and so charming.
Though many colors, they are one;

They sing their song in unison.
Happy, lightly, ever shine on brightly.
You so politely inspire me!

194. If you wish to find out what's in a man, wait to see what comes out of him. (Matthew 12:34).[48]

195. When you use the term "white person" or "black person," I would ask first of all what planet do they come from?

196. If you are raising several small children, what you are in effect doing is programming a series of supercomputers.

197. When you're in a hurry, slow down!

198. Somewhere in the beginning God made man. Sometime thereafter, man made lesser gods to bow down to and worship (Exodus 32:4).[49]

199. When someone has passed away, the only time you should say the words, "I wish that they could be back with us again," is when that person didn't make it into heaven.

200. One can only have what one reaches for.

201. De-mean-or … the kind.

Our Land Is Cursed

Our land is now cursed in earth, sky, and sea.
Man restricted from taking what for him was once free.
Time is now tightening; winding down are our chances.
Man blinded by what he thinks are advances
(Ecclesiastes 1:9).[50]
The earth trembles oft as if God has stepped down,
Displeased at the little righteousness found.
The wind and the flood's violent path in the earth,

Drought, desolation, pestilence, dearth!
Plague and disease grip men in fear,
Who once never think that their Lord might appear
(2 Timothy 4:1).[51]
Our land is now cursed; men kill every day.
Murder's the norm while men seek not nor pray (Matthew 7:7).[52]
New strains of old viruses, our vaccines they resist.
Added trouble and woe against men persist.
Can you see it, oh people? We're engulfed in sin's flame.
Our doom and destruction are but ours to blame.
Our land is now cursed.
The hand writes on the wall (Daniel 5:5).[53]
As our friend Humpty Dumpty, who had his great fall,
Not a single king's horse and none of his men
Could put Humpty back together from sin.
We can heal our land's curse if we seek a way out.
Faith must replace a heart tainted with doubt.
Believe the Lord's Word, accept what he's saying,
That the answer is found on your knees just by praying!
"I'll answer, my child, Hearing each word you say,
And the curse now upon you will be taken away."
Our land that is cursed can be whole once again,
If we surrender our hearts and be cleansed of our sin.
And nature, the elements, will be friend not foe,
If to the Lord daily we humbly would go.
Our land that's now burdened would sigh great relief,
And only because of our heartfelt belief
In God's plan of salvation that has made now a way,
Back to life everlasting if we just learn to pray.

202. A truth not observed or acknowledged by man shines none the less brilliantly before the face of God.

203. Many men harbor a blind confidence that by ignoring the truth it will simply go away (John 18:38; Matthew 27:24).[54]

204. Find the one you love, and you will find satisfaction. Settle now only for the one you want, and you will seek all your life for the one you love.

A complicated little girl named …

Erika

Erika, oh child of woe,
Why did the world it teach you so,
To dwell in darkness, shadows cast,
To live in pain, to live in pain.
Erika, was it not you whose brightened sun was turned to blue?
Where laughter's childhood turned to rain,
Where songfest was not taught to gain.
Oh, Erika, I need you so to understand
What you must know; consider, child, the seeds you sow
Can change your tears to laughter.
Erika, the time has come
To change your world, to change your world
To song, and please believe it so.
Do sow the seeds of faith and know
That he who rules above the best
Will stand you, child, to pass the test,
Will heighten you to tower tall,
Will give you joy and peace and all.
Oh, Erika, I say to you, to Erika be true.

205. Being frank with someone doesn't always mean that your timing is not off.

206. Understanding is the only way one can productively utilize an idea.

207. Hate is a weak man's excuse for not loving.

208. People want to be important because they don't know that they already are (Psalms 8:4).[55]

209. "Thou shalt not steal … Thou shalt not kill … Thou shalt not bear false witness …" Why were these words removed from our public schools?

210. Some of the poorest men on earth have the most money.

211. Marble … chisel … skill: masterpiece!

Kind and tender …
Love Is not Extreme

Love is not extreme,
Is never what it does not seem,
Will never bring you down,
Need not be called to be around,
Will last the course of time.
If man will seek, it's love he'll find.
Will do the things it must,
Is filled with faith and hope and trust.
Always hopes the best for you,
Is devoted and forever true.
Call on it? The answer's, "Yes!"
Stands firm through every trial and test.
Completely on the up and up,
Overflows when God fills up its cup (Psalm 23:5).[56]
Love is not extreme, love is not extreme.

212. Fill your Christmas stockings with gifts for others.

213. If there is something worth finding, seek it!

214. When you don't feel small then bigness opens up to you.

215. The most exiting classrooms are the ones with the most exited teachers.

216. Man is lonely because he needs Jesus to keep him company.

217. In the beginning God created man, ... not the other way around (Genesis 1:27).[57]

218. Most people fear death because they fear hell.

219. Adversity in our lives often fans the winds of positive change (Romans 5:3–5).[58]

220. The individual who puts his trust in material wealth becomes a material being.

221. In order to change one's life, one must introduce an agent of change into his or her life. For to not introduce new things into one's life is to perpetuate the life one wishes to change.

222. The future looks bright only for those who visualize a bright future.

Is it whole or a ...
Peace that Is in Pieces

Peace that's in pieces is not peace at all;
If a man can stand, why then would he fall?
If the daylight is shining, why see we but clouds;
If all the earth is before us, why exist we in crowds?
If the grain is in surplus, why then do men die
For the want of their hunger while the filled pass them by?
If there is a heaven, should not we there dwell?
If we're "bought with a price," do we then our souls sell?
(1 Corinthians 6:20)?[59]
If the morning's before us, why so long is the night?

Why choose to do wrong when we could choose to do right?
If men are born free, why so many in chains?
And if hope's an idea, why do the hopeless remain?
Why try we so hard by our power and might
(Zechariah 4:6),[60]
Struggling in darkness, in the absence of light.
We are born into sin God can wash away
For Jesus proclaimed it, "I am the way!"
For our peace is in pieces, therefore, not peace at all.
God's truth is the life, but the most ignored call
(John 14:6)![61]

223. If good works saved a man, the thief who hung beside Jesus could not have been saved (Luke 23:40–43).[62]

224. Sin's reward is death (Romans 6:23).[63]

225. God does not go back on his word (Matthew 24:35)![64]

226. The man who pays for a pair of shoes with honest money can wear them conscience free. The man, however, who steals that same pair of shoes will still have to pay for them, but the cost will be much greater for him than for the man who bought them with honest money.

227. Garbage and ungodly sort of rhyme, don't they?

228. Words shape our tomorrows.

229. Justice presides in the courtroom only if just men do.

230. If a simple smile can erase an entire frown, just think of what a little love might do.

231. When men praise an evil man, they are not praising the man, they are praising his evil.

232. Inertia is the tendency of a body in motion to remain in motion. So is the man who does not pause from time to time to ponder his path.

Lo Behold and Deep Within

Lo behold and deep within,
I see beneath the surface, in.
So rare it is of things untold,
Unfold, to me, unfold.
Lo behold, the tale I tell,
Bewailing captives lost in hell.
In thee, oh Lord, I find, I wait in faith, for thee I wait.
How do, be I, to now this time,
A righteous ending life to find.
Part the way, the evil dark,
To one day find and then impart
A gentle knocking at my heart.
'Tis Jesus calls … 'Tis Jesus calls.
And never more to loss to be,
Beckons freedom, ah yes, to me!
For lo behold, yes, deep within,
I see beneath the surface in.
So rare it is of things not told
Of life, of love I now behold.
My God, it did to me unfold.

233. Poignant and rhetorical phrases are not always necessary to portray eloquent ideas.

234. The mother who thinks that it is so cute when her two-year-old son hits at her will one day smile with artificial teeth.

235. The magnificent ideas that come from man, don't come from man.

236. Evil men test the good.

237. When the breath is gone from the body, and the soul is silenced from the earth, then is impressed upon that soul the reality of that world he or she thought only to be fantasy.

238. The woman said arrogantly one day, "God never said anything to me!" A few minutes later, not noticing the workman's "caution" sign, she walked into an open ditch, nearly killing herself.

239. A person can see no further than what they think.

Oh ache … oh pain …
Oh, Jealous Heart

Oh, jealous heart, oh, empty gain,
Your night has made me so
To leave behind the things of peace,
The things I used to know.
Oh, jealousy, vile, and barren child,
I wake in pain each day.
Life's sweetness stranded; what bitter pill
For I've no love to give away.
Oh, jealous heart, with stealth you take
And take till I've no more.
No average thoughts, no simple things,
No things that I adore.
Oh, jealousy, oh, vengeful judge,
Steep sentence you bestow.
And drain me of my precious life
Till I am kept in hell below.
Oh, jealous heart, you poison me,
And this, oh, jealous heart, I know.

240. You find only what you seek. You seek only what you imagine you can find.

241. The fact that anything at all is establishes the fact that something always was.

242. The weight of a person's words are the actions that follow them (James 2:20).[65]

243. The eyes of a child are his or her parents.

244. So you thought no one saw you do that.

245. When I found out that a snake has no eyelids, it was then I understood how it is that Satan never sleeps.

246. What you don't want to know you never will.

247. *Now* is both the present and the future.

248. It's easy to die in your sins.

249. Every time you open your mouth, you tell on yourself.

250. To love is to do what love does (1 Corinthians 13:4).[66]

I am no longer here, I am …
Gone a Far Journey

Gone a far journey to my long home away;
Gone a far journey … gone in one day.
Contained in an instant, as a vapor was I (James 4:14),[67]
Cast now from life's earth when death drew me nigh.
Gone a far journey, marks the tick-tock of time;
Death wrapped in life's mysterious rhyme.
Gone I by midnight, I'll never return,
Whether my lot is rejoicing or my lot is to burn.
Gone away sinner, if that be thy name,
Outcast of God will never perish thy flame.
Or … received of redemptive power and love,
Thy being rejoicing in the forever above.
Gone, and thy journey is over and done.
Gone, for thy battle's lost or it's won.
Gone away trouble … or ever present thy grief,
You're gone away faithless or gone away in belief.

Gone a far journey to my long home away;
Gone a far journey … gone in one day.
Contained in an instant, as a vapor was I,
Cast now from life's earth when death drew me nigh.
Gone a far journey … gone away, gone away …

251. Thoughts are held in the mind, opinions in the heart.

252. There was a man who, for years, only thought he was seeking Jesus until the day the Lord came to his front door in the form of a person in need (Matthew 7:21).[68]

253. Corporations are protected; people are not.

We have become …

A World of Strangers

A world of strangers are not as one,
And avoid each others eyes.
They know not and care not to seek
Their brother's cause or to hear his cries.
A world of strangers, faceless pods,
Know not what it means to touch.
Caring more for animals …
For men? Not half as much.
A world of strangers who still ignore
The cry of the oppressed.
Who do not know their God doth watch
And that they fail his every test.
A world of strangers, heartless faces
Who every day declare,
"Our brothers perish from the earth,
And we don't even care."

254. The man who loves all kinds of women will one day join all kinds of women who loved all kinds of men … in hell.

One bothersome grain yields …
The Oyster's Pearl

The oyster's pearl does symbolize
The rough in life, but then the prize;
For in its shell a grain of sand
Does irritate it to no end.
But in coping with its daily strife
Brings forth rare beauty from its life,
A costly pearl, both pure and true,
Lovely, lasting, and precious, too.
The rough in life may come our way,
But for this cause do not dismay.
Just weather the troubles of this world,
And you will emerge a precious pearl.

255. Eternal damnation is too huge a concept to toy with when contemplating the eventual *resting place* of your eternal soul.

Much can be seen …
Even in the Darkness

Even in the darkness there is light.
On the dim path there is bright.
In bitterness there is sweet,
Though learning is a rough road, it finds a peaceful retreat
(1 Peter 4:12–13).[69]

In the sad times there is joy
For tears will fall when we destroy
The works of death and sin,
Before new life in us begins.
In losing there is gain;
In being stripped sometimes the best remains.
Even in the darkness there is light,
And the soon disappearance of an endless night.

256. That which is done in secret will soon be known in public (Luke 8:17).[70]

257. The atheist demonstrates the profound belief that there is a God through emphatic denial that one exists! Those who truly don't believe that there is a God never bring his name up.

258. Jesus said, "Fear not." What exactly did he mean when he said that? "Fear … not" (Matthew 10:28).[71]

It's the product of an idea, but …
It Starts with a Dream

It starts with a dream; it starts with belief,
With little things that soon increase.
It starts with acceptance; it starts with, "I will."
Just clear out your mind, look at one thought, be still (Psalm 46:10).[72]
It starts with reality, which is what you believe,
For what's clear in your mind is what you perceive.
It starts with a dream, and one you can find,
Your skies can be blue if you leave doubt behind.
So dream, dream, my child, whether five or one hundred.
When your mind is still active your thoughts can be thundered!

It starts with a dream, stand, believe, oh child, know
God is controlling all of Earth's things below.
To gain the increase, it starts with belief. It starts with a dream.

259. Well-behaved children come from well-behaved homes.

260. Among mankind's greatest assets are the friends he has yet to meet.

261. Flattery is how a real snake charms its victim (Proverbs 7:21).[73]

262. Prayer, as a practice, when faithfully exercised, opens doors to those things that are prayed for (Mark 11:23–24).[74]

263. Reach into your head sometime, and see what kind of new ideas you can pull out.

264. I see into your heart through your eyes.

265. The man who *wants* does not know that the Lord is his shepherd (Psalm 23:1).[75]

266. The only thing that prevents someone from succeeding is the unwillingness to.

267. Love loves all equally.

Life and death are part of a mysterious cycle because …

As It Sets, It's Rising

Whenever the sun sets, it is also rising;
Death and rebirth are as one.
As one's breath drawn—its last—it's inspired anew;
Through death's veil no one can see.
As God's sun is a setting chased by a purplish hue,
Teardrops are falling, are falling …
Whenever the sun sets, it is also rising,
And another dawn is beginning anew.

268. In the haste of accomplishing personal and ambitious goals, one often passes the most important things in life by.

269. The uncontrolled tongue is not uncontrolled (James 3:5–6).[76]

270. Though I possess money, but my life bears no meaningful message; the money I possess becomes pointless.

271. Nothing in existence passes unseen before the eyes of God.

272. There is right and then there is an individual's opinion of what he or she thinks is right.

273. Someone who runs for this nation's highest office just because he or she wants to be president is not fit to hold that office.

274. A land is not free until it is free from sin.

275. Leaders have the knack for exciting others about their ideas.

276. When David had nowhere else to go, he turned to the Lord. David had nowhere else to go a lot.

277. Prayer heads trouble off at the pass.

278. To "go with the flow" reminds me of a man in a paddleless canoe, drifting toward the edge of Niagara Falls.

Many unexplained things are clearly seen …
Beyond the Veil

Beyond the veil, beyond the mist,
There lies a tale of hidden bliss,
Where marriage, heart, of soul and mind,
And gifted things marvelous in design.
Beyond in truth where psyche see,
Where tailor-made, where all things be.
Once stripped of self, its tainted view,
What's manifest appears in you.
Beyond the veil, beyond the mist
Lies hidden bliss.

279. Money can buy some of the best things in the world that money can buy, but none of the best things in the world that money can't buy.

280. It is belief in the difficulty of a thing that makes the difficult thing difficult.

281. Every question that modern science answers leads to deeper questions that modern science then must answer. This leaves many questions unanswered by modern science.

282. "I can't," is identicle to, "I won't." "I won't" means, "I will not." "I will not," means not that I can't but that I refuse to!

283. The value of knowledge lies in its use.

284. If a UFO is unidentified, why do some people assume that it comes from outer space?

285. No matter what the situation looks like, God is looking at it, too.

286. When the angels of the Lord and the angels of the Devil engage in war, there may be a battle, but there is no contest (Revelation 12:7).[77]

287. The selfish man is like a wealthy man in a world with no people.

288. The human eye cannot see faith.

289. The body itself is a complex, intelligent being.

290. To seriously hinder an evil spirit, lift your own.

One day …
David Died

David died, just like that.
No plans were made; no bags were packed.
In one grim day his life was gone
To the unknown vast, that place beyond.
David left with no good-byes,
Just cut away, to our surprise.
We have but what we pictured last

Contained in our dim memory's grasp.
David bid no one farewell;
his life did its short story tell.
To "fade-a-way …" and "dis … appear,"
And David was no longer here.
Our lives, as David's, come and go,
And very little meaning shows.
For one day this thing, the next day that,
Then comes to be our closing act.
Farewell, our David passed away.
In judgment does his poor soul lay;
Our fleeting moment as a vapor ends (James 4:14)[78]
Before eternal life begins …
Or eternal death, so dismal, dark,
When Satan steals away our heart.
Did he steal what beat inside
Of David's soul, of David's pride?
For David's gone, farewell today.
No more to laugh; no more to pray.
And David died, just like that
With no plans made, with no bags packed.
In one grim day his life was gone
To the unknown vast, beyond.
You will, in a moment, be no more
And touch, as David, some distant shore.
But know, please this, as loved ones cry,
You will, one day, as David, die.

291. If I love you and don't show it, then I don't love you.

292. The games that small children play are part of their serious world.

293. God turns questions into answers.

294. A handful of people (artistic critics) cannot judge the public will.

295. Without a purpose, why get out of bed in the morning?

296. For those who feel that it is impossible to touch a thought, I offer you this: just reach out and touch anything of the world's material substance, and you have just touched a thought (Hebrews 11:1).[79]

297. People who throw trash out of their car window, or into the nearest sewer outlet, actually think that's going to make it go away.

298. Universal truths are stated in many forms and in many ways by many people, but they are still the same universal truths.

299. The local tavern was designed for three things:

    A. To take your money

    B. To take time you could be putting to better use

    C. And to distract you until your soul is finally taken, too

300. A person's ability to earn a living has many times been erased by "accident."

As I climb in the spirit, I know that …
My Star Is Rising

I stand in awe, and as I dream,
The life I live I only seem.
The time is spent, but that is passed.
The joy I've had, why can't it last?
But now I see, I peer within,
that life itself can now begin.
My star is rising, I feel its glow,
my heart affirms and says it's so.
The dreams displayed upon my soul,
have placed me on toward my goal.
My star is rising, so clean, so free.
My star is just the risen me!

301. Even the short and seemingly insignificant life span of an insect is filled with purpose.

302. As the motorist pressed the pedal to the metal, he only managed arriving all too quickly at the next stop sign.

Warm love in a …
Wedding Summer

Wedding summer, when mate my soul did
with nuptial bliss,
And mated soul affirmed its union with
admiration's first kiss.
Southerly breezes embraced my cold
and shallow past,
Dismissing the old for things new.
It was in life's summer that I found the wedding,
and in the marriage, I found you.

303. David had a little something "extra" with him that had nothing to do with the stones in his pouch.

304. In regard to parts of speech, "love" is an action verb.

A Little Town Called Bethlehem

In a little town called Bethlehem, a miracle took place;
The plan was human misery from our world to be erased.
The plan had been conceived by God,
for when he made the world he'd known
That man would turn away from him

and have his blessings overthrown.
But hark, in little Bethlehem the miracle conceived
Was Jesus, begotten Son of God,
by the world to be received.
But lo, these many, many years, very few have taken in
The miracle of Bethlehem so that brand-new life begins.
The miracle, the miracle, hark, the angels glad proclaim
That Jesus, blessed Prince of Peace,
is a name above all names!
The miracle of Bethlehem, oh, blessed song of peace,
This wonder adds those precious things
that love, that love increase!
Have you a town called Bethlehem abiding in your heart?
Just wish upon the star that led the wise men to the ox's ark,
That little stable tucked away in yonder's little town,
Thank God for little Bethlehem,
whose fame did earth surround.
Oh, Bethlehem, oh, Bethlehem,
your little soul did ease our hearts,
And because our God did deem it so,
your legacy will not depart
Till men are free from prison's sin,
till men are free to heed life's call,
That they must, too, give up their hearts,
as the Son of God gave up his all (John 3:16).[80]
In a little town called Bethlehem,
eternal life did sound its voice
So that all one day might ascend on high
and with Jesus Christ rejoice!

305. There is no event in the human experience over which the permissive will of God does not preside.

306. The kingdom of God is rich in everything.

307. What one hates indicates what one fears.

308. Doubt creates reasons for not believing.

309. Some of the best medicines in the world are the worst tasting.

310. When one's desire wanders, it is because the heart is out of place.

311. Poison is usually the unseen component in the mixture.

312. To understand an individual's motives, just pay attention to the things they overlook in the quest to attain their goals.

313. The man who does not know himself, studies his questions. The man who does know himself, studies his answers.

314. To long for and hold on to the memory of one's youth is to frustrate one's present and deny one's future.

315. The heart is often visited by strange ideas draped in dark designs.

316. Spirits that do not agree are instantly at war.

317. It is the thought behind it that gives a word its form.

318. Sin if you like; it's the consequences of sin you will not like (Romans 6:23).[81]

319. Carpenters are known by the way they carry their tools.

320. Sometimes the Lord will have us cross a sea whose dry path is not yet open to us.

321. You will pay for it.

322. Fix the problem.

323. All good thoughts come from above. All evil thoughts come from below. So it necessarily follows that our thoughts are never our own (James 1:17).[82]

When I behold your beauty …
My Eyes Are Filled with You

My eyes are filled with you,
So full and so completely.
Your presence sets my world aglow;
I marvel how discreetly.
I need you when you are not there,
But when my eyes behold you,
My mind is chased of every care,
My eyes are filled with you.

324. Before the outcome of a matter is known, let prayer surround and persuade it.

325. Sure, make waves—positive ones!

326. Human space exploration rhymes with "man's vain imagination."

327. How many people this year know that they are not going to live to see next year?

328. Aren't you tired of the human r-a-c-e?

329. The strength of the laws of any land are tested when any of the least of them are broken (Matthew 5:19).[83]

330. Adam followed his woman into sin (Genesis 3:6, 7).[84]

331. Who knows tomorrow?

332. When you see doctors, lawyers, and other people on accomplished professional levels, you are seeing what all young people can one day be.

333. The aim of modern medicine is to *manage* disease, not cure it.

334. Once attained, fame's momentum is easily maintained.

335. The next time there is too little of something to go around, just imagine it to be two fishes and five loaves of bread (Matthew 14:17–21).[85]

They've faded away …
The Roses Have Turned

The roses have turned; they are sullen and gray.
Their beauty has wilted, has faded away.
They're gone a far journey, in a new home to be,
No more gracing others by their beauty but free.
The roses have turned quite away to the side,
To a new home, there, to always abide.
The roses have turned; their earthly bodies dissolved.
In the scheme of God's plan, life's travel mystery is solved.
The roses have turned, and though sullen and gray,
Claim a being more beautiful in their home far away.
The roses have turned into beauty; they rest,
Having given to others' lives always their best.

336. The man who entertains unsaintly thoughts toward his neighbor's wife has committed adultery with her already in his heart (Matthew 5:27, 28).[86]

337. Man, unlike a dog, can learn new tricks at any age.

338. When discussing one's plans with others, it is more often wise not to.

339. The laws of the land are a strict reminder that God does not compromise or allow anyone to "slip" by any of his.

340. A man thinks. A woman feels.

341. No army on earth can stop a man from dreaming!

342. Many voices cry, "Pro-choice," as they slaughter the innocent who have none.

343. In order to reach a goal, think of it as inevitable, and keep it fresh in your mind.

344. The quality of your education is based on the quality of its instruction.

345. If God had meant for men to live separate and apart from one another, he would have put them on different planets!

346. Filthy rich: with so many poor, needy, and destitute in the world, think about what that means.

347. Why reach for the unattainable?

My home? …
America

I gaze across the waves and waves of people grain.
The purple mountains there unseen,
That stand so statuesque and yet
Deny themselves, deny themselves.
The pollinated wondrous plains
That wave so steadily about;
Swept away is doubt that I can be
As grand as they are, as they are to me.
America, God has shed his grace on thee
And placed a crown of brotherhood on all thy good.
America, my tears I shed, my tears I shed for thee.
For spaciousness of amber skies,
I hear the people as they cry.
America, would you deny the cry of the oppressed?
And in the wake of liberty,
Tear-filled eyes that yearn to see
Thy precious bell begin to ring
And cause thy people now to sing,

America, the beautiful … our land of peace …
Land of the free …
America, one day will be
America to me.

Play gently to me your music …

Oh, Rainy Day

Oh rainy day, my comfort friend,
Oh rainy day, please do not end.
Oh rainy day, do ere remain,
And rain and rain and rain and rain!

348. What a man finds in a bar is usually what he was looking for.

349. Men who hate themselves find ways to hurt themselves. Men who hurt themselves rarely understand that it is because they hate themselves.

The prince of darkness has …

Fallen

Fallen angel, woe art thou
whose empty threat sought empty power.
Felled thee from thy honored place,
Fell miles from heaven through empty space
To hell beneath twix flame and fire.
From agony you'll not retire.
Thy darkness there will always be,
Bound, ashamed … never free.
All thy tomorrows, the same lost doom,

And grief thy soul will ere consume.
How could you think to be above
Your creator, your master, a God of love
(Isaiah 14:12–15)?[87]
Fallen angel, felled from grace,
From position, from beauty, to a dim disgrace.
No hope is thine that thou return;
Thy lot is to forever burn.
Lofty Lucifer held high,
God-given rank in times gone by.
Now ruined Serpent let men escape
By obedience to God your cursed fate.

I often desire that the Lord would …

Steal Me Away

Steal me away to the evening places;
Steal me away to the quiet of calm;
Steal me away to the billowing white clouds
That hold me so softly in their billowing arms.
Steal me away to the quiet of tranquil;
Steal me away to the tender of love.
Steal me away to the ever of lasting,
Steal me away to my God's great above.

She left suddenly, and I cried out to her …

Mother, Mother

Mother, Mother, gone'd away,
Away was whisked thy soul today.
Away, unearthed from earthly pain,
In heaven's safety realm you will remain.

My insides emptied now of thee,
Where once thy love surrounded me.
Mother, Mother, I long the day
When I, my soul, too, is whisked away.

350. As is the mountain that is full of gold and precious stones, so is the heart that is full of good things to say.

351. Talking to God is a simple act … of faith.

352. When a man worries about his age, it is not his age that he is worried about.

353. To snag a fish, the hook must be barbed. To win a soul for Christ, the barbed hook must be love (Matthew 4:19).[88]

354. When one grows older, it is sad indeed when one does not grow wiser.

In the terrible day of judgment …
Many Cowards Will Be Told

Many cowards will be told.
Many a failed heart will every eye behold.
Many a quivering soul not free.
Many the lost in judgment will be.
Many the quaking when Gabriel's trumpet will sound …
Many wanting in the balance, found.
Many cowards in that day will be told,
But the righteous will be bold.

355. Man, himself, is responsible for his sins. (Psalm 51:4)[89]

356. An education at least gives you options.

357. In some cases, if you want to find something, stop looking for it, and it will soon find you.

358. Rain is rarely selective on whom it falls. (Matthew 5:45)[90]

359. One who ignores his neighbor's pain will one day experience it.

360. Eternal life won't cost you much ... just the world (Matthew 16:25).[91]

Come ...
Taste

Taste the grace; erase the pain.
With knowledge wisdom came.
Climb the mountain, scale the dream.
The blood of Jesus thy soul redeem.
Tuck far from sin, love with thy best.
Pass, oh man, the test!
For by God's love he sent his grace,
and from thee a doubtful outcome chased.

361. A corrupt nation will inherit corrupt leadership.

362. When God forms a baby in its mother's womb, he also forms the selectest of milk in her breasts to nourish that baby. My question is, what does man's formula have over God's formula that it would feign to replace it?

363. Each lost youth is but another lost seed of hope for an already failing humanity.

364. In the hour of decision, the man who is afraid to make one dies a little.

365. Time is a concept.

366. A person who grows old is one whose thoughts have ceased to multiply.

367. Time is running out.

368. Mom, dad, and the kids: the most simple form of government.

369. The masses are a control experiment.

370. Faith is man's power tool.

371. Pray now or pay later.

372. You don't need something to end up with something (Hebrews11:1).[92]

373. Art is more what a person "sees" than what a person paints.

374. The road ahead is your road.

375. "The end of time" speaks simply of the end of *your* time here on earth.

376. One reaches only the height of what he or she dreams.

377. When Pontius Pilate dipped his hands in the bowl, he did not wash away the guilt of his judgment against Christ.

378. Every poor man on earth, at any moment, is rich in opportunity.

379. Wisdom is a source of drink hidden deep in the earth that must be carefully sought out, skillfully and patiently dug into, and once found, continually drawn from for its substance is life.

380. A beautiful body needs a beautiful mind to go with it.

381. Ship without a helm? Man with no moral compass.

382. Togetherness? … The horn section!

383. The modern food industry provides, in surplus, non nutritional foods that starve the body, weaken its immune system, infuse it with deadly chemicals, leaving it susceptible to disease and eventual death.

The modern marriage today is most times …
A Modern Bore

A wedding ring once meant so much
Upon the hand that wore it;
A man and woman married did
their life as one adore it.
But now it seems that ring is just a figure of the past,
For modern couples of today rarely ever last.
Their love springs up on stony ground
And withers in the heat of day (Mark 4:16, 17)[93]
Because their love did not take root
before they gave their vows away.
So stands the ring more meaningless than ever was before,
So the modern marriage turns out to be most times a modern bore.

Is the impossible possible? …
That's What Faith Will Do for You
(Hebrews 11:1)[94]

Give to you your dream come true,
Make real the things that only seem,
Will open doors and bring you through
And land you safe within your dreams.
Will build for you a house of gold,
Provide your every need,
If you'll but with the faithful hold
To that tiny grain of mustard seed.
Make you joyful, though the world be sad,
Tuck you in the bed of peace,
Will give you things you never had;
Your every care will be released.

Will land you safe through desert sands,
Will make of you brand new,
Place you safely in the Master's hands,
That's what faith will do for you.

384. Save what you have, and you'll have what you save.

385. An empire built by an individual will be passed on to others.

386. When we say that something makes us mad, that can't be true because God already made us, and he didn't make us mad.

387. Unconscionable acts exact unthinkable punishments.

388. The army that rises to oppress will one day be forgotten.

389. A jackleg electrician might very well burn your house down. How so? By the construct of wiring that is not according to an established code, or by the use of materials not suitable to bear the proper load. The same is true for the nation whose government has displaced well-established and existing laws thwarting the common principles of God.

390. The death of many a relationship has been announced by the words, "I need my space."

391. Apathy is desireless.

392. Soap cleans the outside. Repentance cleans the inside (1 Corinthians 6:11).[95]

393. Every spring God makes clear to all, the resurrection of the dead.

394. An individual studies life from the classroom of his or her own heart.

So peacefully laid upon the hillside are the …
Gravestones Strewn

Gravestones strewn
in the place where they were laid to rest.
Gravestones set atop a grassy carpet bed …
And in the depth where they did sink
the body that remained behind.
The thought most uttered in their hearts
Is with what body did that soul emerge,
in yonder land, what kind
(1 Corinthians 15:53)?[96]
Gravestones that mark ages past,
gravestones that mark passage to
The mystery that lies ahead,
break'd from the life that now is through.
Gravestones strewn apart and near,
but when the souls depart, I hear
A resting place and hell betwixt,
a great nonpassage gulf is fixed.
Gravestones testify though still;
make straight thine heart, and firm thy will!
When your body's sunk into the ground,
oh where, oh man, will thy soul be found?
Among the gravestones strewn apart?
Or waked to find damnation's true.
I think it wise to prepare thine heart,
for death means not the end of you.
For far beneath the gravestones strewn apart,
And far beneath their grassy carpet bed,
There's a hell beneath and a throne on high,
And God before which are judged the dead.
I see the gravestones white, rose, and gray,
laid upon that field of green.
They are monuments to the living, not the dead,

Of heaven and earth; their message is fixed in between.
They speak their solemn yet unspoken message stern.
Their words, though silent, are for us to learn,
Wherein only the silent hearts
of men can be found to be true,
That you will meet your end in fears or joy
when this life journey's through.
So when you see gravestones strewn about,
in a field so silent and laid so calm,
Remember what remains of you will lay there, too.
But your awareness will to another field be gone ...
Far beyond those gravestones that are strewn apart,
And far beyond their grassy carpet bed.
The message in them does address itself to
Those who are living, and not to the dead.
The gravestones declare, and do silently say
To prepare, meet thy maker, and do not delay!

395. A "prayer raised" is called "pray-raise" or "praise."

396. The Devil is a lost soul, looking for company.

397. As the physical body ages, the spiritual man does not.

398. When children do not get what they need from mom and dad, they
spend their entire lives trying to get it from someone else.

I See Them as Angels

I see them as angels, standing about.
In the unseen invisible, they are present, no doubt.
Their existence is known to the faithful who view;
The things they accept and believe to be true.
I see them as angels, regimental they stand.

More mighty than mortals, their excellence, grand,
They wait in obedience on their God from above.
His might is all power; his wisdom is love.
I see them so lofty, yet beside me they are.
Though instant their rescue, they come from afar.
I see them as angels and for all men a guide;
That they're sent from God's presence cannot be denied.
For I see them as angels. I see them as angels.

399. Children are taught by what they see you do.

400. Billboards project ideas that are powered by suggestion.

401. Had any good ideas lately? Who do you think gave them to you? … God.

402. Easter has nothing to do with bunnies or egg hunts.

They are …

Parked in Caverns of the Night

Parked in caverns of the night,
The dead are waiting there,
Parked and deeply out of sight.
Oh, traveler beware
For when you walk where darkness looms,
You place yourself in jeopardy,
And Satan would your soul consume,
He, mixed with night you cannot see.

403. A license to drive does not give you a license to drive recklessly. By the same token, authority does not give you a license for its misuse.

404. The same bombs that an unjustified government drops so willingly on other countries will one day be dropped on it, even if they are not in the form of bombs.

405. The things that a man yields his heart to, good or bad, are also the things he ends up with in his life, good or bad.

406. The individual who gives expecting something back in return has not given (Matthew 5:47).[97]

407. Sweetness tasted by the soul is hard to forget.

Don't think of them as gone …
Loved Ones Passed

Loved ones passed, but are they gone?
My heart alone doth sigh.
They are not dead; they're gone to rest.
I need not question why.
Our precious Savior died one day,
So there would one day be
A home of rest for every soul
To dwell eternally.
They are not dead; they're going home
To tender, mellow skies.
Your loved ones have reached happy shores.
Now dry your weeping eyes (Revelation 7:17).[98]

408. Thinking without feeling is like power without love.

409. You may not always see what's going on, but what's going on (and on) sees you.

410. A broad base offers more support.

411. Can life die?

412. All men dream.

413. An insult only harms the insulted.

414. If he does not see himself in a poor light, the poor man is not truly poor.

415. Test-tube babies are not test-tube babies.

416. Same God, different day.

417. A city is built one brick at a time.

418. The man said to his brother, "I am willing, now, to bury the hatchet." So when his brother turned and started to walk away, he buried it in his back.

419. It's the extra things you put in the pot that give it taste.

420. Ticktock, ticktock, tick … eternity (Mark 3:29).[99]

421. The Bible in a courtroom was always a witness against those who swore on it (Matthew 5:33–37).[100]

Heavenly beings invite you into …
The Happy Doorway

The happy doorway, now open brings
Many blessed and saintly things.
The happy doorway of the sheepfold to
(John 10:1),[101]
Reveals the law, the right, the true.
The happy doorway has one way in,
Invites the soul that's free from sin.
The happy doorway is Jesus Christ,
And to all who come, eternal life.

422. The heart of a compassionate soul is moved to many charitable acts (Luke 6:19).[102]

423. If you raise hell here on earth, you will raise hell in eternity ... the level of its population, that is (Isaiah 5:14).[103]

424. Men follow outward maps, seeking inward treasures (Luke 17:20, 21, 22).[104]

425. The proud embrace the illusion of having power over other people.

426. When one's life ends, one's eternal life begins.

427. A man's needs are not always his wants.

428. On the day Jesus died on Calvary, there was such a concentration of invisible beings gathered in that one place, contesting the possession of his body, that they blotted out the sun.

429. Love will never leave you (Matthew 28:20).[105]

430. If a man were to truly tap into himself, he would find God there. (Luke 17:20,21)[106]

431. A letter of complaint written by the wealthy carries a lot of weight.

432. Need a little love in your life? Try lov ... ing.

Why wait. It is better to ...

Seek It Now

Seek thy soul's eternal rest,
Seek it from within;
Seek salvation's peaceful stream,
And let good fortune's dream begin.
Seek not bitter but the sweet;
seek it now, today.
Tomorrow just might be too late;
by then, life's breath might steal away.

433. When you don't finish your work, you don't enjoy your play as much.

434. A community's police department is its watchman upon the wall (Psalm 127:1).[107]

435. The mind is more excellent than any of its inventions.

What Is Love?

What is love; is love blue?
What is love; is love true?
What is time? Time is spent.
Time I spent, days loving you.
What is true? Love is true.
What is, "I am loving you"?
It is time spent, love so true.
It is love spent loving you.

436. After death some return to dust … others return to Jesus.

437. Without sufficient calcium in the body, the bones become weak and are easily broken. So, too, is the child in whose life no discipline is applied.

438. A child may be too young to understand certain things, but his or her little mind still absorbs everything it sees.

Through all our years together, still …
I Love You So

I loved you so with flowers blooming.
I loved you so when leaves were green.

I loved you so when leaves were falling,
and also with them no more seen.
I loved you so through all life's season's,
As things were changed about.
I loved you for life's many reasons.
Of this I know you have no doubt.
And I love you now though leaves are blooming,
Or green or falling down,
My love is true and ever, darling.
My love is you and so profound.

439. One day a man proclaimed insolently, "There is no God!" On another day, shortly thereafter, his heart suddenly stopped beating. Those who came upon his lifeless body said that they could see in those dead eyes an expression of great surprise.

440. A man's soul is his real body.

441. Vision sees tomorrow the way it sees today—as present and existing.

442. There is only one battle, and it belongs to the Lord (1 Samuel 17:47).[108]

443. You never end.

444. In America, he who has the most money orders the rest of us around.

445. The answer is there … right beside you (Exodus 4:2).[109]

446. It is a foolish man, indeed, who is willing to face eternity unprepared to die!

447. If it's your body and you declare your right to control it, why can't you stop it from making a baby?

448. Fishing is the art of waiting. Waiting is the art of fishing.

449. A friend found is a treasure discovered whose value will never diminish.

450. Some time ago I was spoken to by an angel of the Lord who said to me, "In hell there is no tomorrow."

451. To the carpenter a hammer is valuable, necessary, and important to the execution of his craft. In life, to the average person, money is valuable, necessary, and important in their lives. The carpenter, however, unlike the average person, does not bow down to and worship his hammer as he would a god.

452. "Seat belts secured?" You'll wish you had, or others who love you will wish you had.

453. The biggest star I ever met was Jesus. You know, the bright and morning one (Revelation 22:16)?[110]

454. Are you sure … that you are saved?

455. What is the difference between a loan shark and most lending institutions? One charges a "slightly" higher interest rate.

456. A poor man is a man who does not dream.

457. Clever mixtures of words are often pointless chatter.

458. If love doesn't pay the bills, then by whose love are you allowed the strength and ability to work?

At our mother's passing, for you …
Your Four Sons: A Tribute … Mom

Risen to a blessed sunrise,
Lift ye up, O Mother, dear.
Glad you're with our blessed Savior,
Though we wish you still were here.
Here to mingle life within us;
Here to see us safe, tucked in,
For you were forever with us
From where our lives did first begin.
But life's beginning for you now, Mother,

Life in God's sweet dream'd realm.
Heavenly forever chorus,
And joy o'er you ever overwhelm.
We'll see you in the sweet forever
For God did lift you up to be
Our risen mother with our King Jesus,
Who'll care for you eternally.

459. Play—like too much sugar in one's diet, too much play sets up an unhealthy balance in one's personality.

460. Pain carves out a space in one's soul for renewal.

We are in the world …
All Colors Together

All colors together, every man as a friend,
Harmonious lives from beginning to end.
Whether red, white, or brown be the terms that men use,
All nations as one, who'll not each other abuse.
All colors together; let's see all men eat.
Let's disease, war, and poverty in this day defeat!
The human family is one, not for the worst, for the better.
God designed us to be on earth,
All colors together!

461. Ever wake up out of a dream and were glad that you did? Better pay attention to that one.

462. Sharing what one has with others is the same as giving to yourself.

We've all heard the saying, "It's only the tip of the iceberg." This refers to an object whose total mass is primarily unseen. In science, it is suggested that only a small portion of the ability of a man's mind is ever utilized. It stands, therefore, that the individual minds of humanity are as …

Icebergs Deep

The tip of life, but icebergs deep
do murky waters keep.
Submerged in dark, unconscious sleep.
The tip but airs a fractioned life,
Thy only shore, the beach of strife.
What not for peace would I sacrifice?
Then let the mighty iceberg rise
Upward, on toward the skies.
Receive thy unimagined prize!
So many tips but icebergs deep,
Do murky sleeping minds still keep.
Wake up, oh soul, I will repeat,
Wake up from thy unconscious deep.

463. The word "trust" (in the Lord) requires that a man lean not to his own conclusions (Proverbs 3:5, 6).[111]

464. When one dies in his or her sins, so do all their hopes.

465. Parents must cultivate their children as does the farmer his field.

466. Only a foolish man will ask God to forgive him for what he is about to do.

467. When one's mind changes, so does the expression in their eyes.

It is because I love you that …
My Heart Is Throbbing

My heart is throbbing, but not in pain.
Your heart is throbbing, too.
My heart is throbbing love's refrain
For it throbs me to you.
My heart is throbbing happiness
For it can plainly see
Your heart is throbbing y-e-s
For it throbs you to me.

468. In competitive sports, everybody wants to win, but what?

469. A once-created living soul always is.

The lost are still not free …
At Two O'clock

At two o'clock, when bars are closing
And Satan's hand is slight withdrawn,
The partygoers begin disbanding,
Their bottled spirits abruptly gone.
At two o'clock night's tide is changing,
The now bewitched do pumpkins be.
At two o'clock the ball is over,
With many souls still lost,
with many souls not free.

470. That person who can "do no wrong" often does.

471. Reach into your heart sometimes, and take a good look at what you feel.

472. A man's hopes turned over to God are returned to him only not in the form of hopes.

If you have a voice ...
Speak to Me

Speak to me of love and beauty;
Speak to me of truth and peace.
Speak to me of all things truly,
Of an earth where troubles all have ceased.
Speak your mind if comely, gentle;
Speak your mind if pure and clear;
Speak of Jesus's love around us,
Speak of him, and I will hear.
Tell profoundly; don't hold back
The things that kind hearts will receive,
For kind hearts live from things divinely,
And once they hear, they will believe.

473. Jesus ... Satisfaction guaranteed!

474. Where there is envy, that heart has failed the love test.

475. As an automobile without a motor, so is a man without a positive will to drive him.

476. Though people deny and ignore the existence of God, it seems to be his name that they remember to cry out first when sudden calamity strikes.

477. The man who gains more understanding than he had before grows into bigger worlds.

478. Paying your bills on time is a discipline.

479. If you want to know what type of instruction a three-year-old little girl has been given, just listen to the things she tells her doll.

The Spirit of God is …
Rising in the East

Rising in the East, into your window it peeps.
Your soul, it nudges as into your dreams, it creeps.
"Awaken," it urges, "to another of days
Unlike any other of the great ones I've made!"
Awake from your slumber, be wise, oh man, see
That the Father has given salvation for free!
The day star approaches; there will be no delay (Revelation 22:16),[112]
For its Son is the truth, and the life, and the way
(John 14:6).[113]
Rising in the East, its dominion to claim,
Destroying its enemies from ancient time's fame
(Psalm 136:10–15[114]).
It's rising, it's rising, o'er hill, and o'er dale,
O'er mountain, o'er ocean, his holy wings have set sail!
Conquering and to conquer, putting to silence all foes,
Cast down forever in the infernal below.
Prepare ye, make ready, oh man out of time,
For the lack of decision is your life's greatest crime (Joshua 24:15)![115]
In the East he is rising, and in judgment you'll cry,
My soul chose not Jesus, now forever I die!

480. Those who adopt a wait-and-see attitude about everything lack vision.

481. Man's heart is a house of mysteries (Jeremiah 17:9).[116]

482. Growth is the painful separation of oneself from the will of self.

483. Man's dreams are his ladder to the sky!

Young people often think to themselves …

I Have Time, I Have Time, I Have Time

Timeful turning twist of fate,
But for my friend, a twist too late.
His time was now fulfilled below,
But to his knowledge, he did not know.
He, like most on earth, rehearsed the rhyme,
"I have time, I have time, I have time."
But now on earth he can't be found,
And only days ago walked he on the ground.
We laughed and talked; he shared my space.
But now from God's earth he has been erased.
It is only now I recall the day
An old man on the street did say,
"My boys, seek the Lord while he may yet be found,
Before you're buried in the ground.
When you plan your life and set your course,
Please live a life that he'll endorse.
If you'll seek the Lord while it is day,
He'll wash your every sin away."
Why must it come to times of woe
That we seek the Lord and to him we go?
When things are smooth and times seem great,
Consider we not that our time may be growing late?
Yes, my friend is dead, but I'll not cry,
And I won't even question why.
But my God I will seek while life is yet mine,
Never saying again I have time, I have time, I have time.

484. Death is not losing your life; death is losing your soul.

485. The angels of God are terrible in their might.

486. If a man would give up everything for the love of one woman, just think of all he would do if he loved everybody!

487. Jealousy is sick, sad, and violent.

488. Life unfolds like a gorgeous flower, bearing the seeds of infinite tomorrows.

489. As an ostrich buries her head in the sand, so is the individual who refuses to give equal time in thoughts on the subject of death and the hereafter.

I am sealed ...

In His Envelope

In his envelope I am sealed,
Many undiscovered sights revealed.
In the clasping of his certainty,
A once captive soul's no more claimed to be.
Inside me is placed his most Holy Word.
Now, throughout the world, I am a voice ... heard.
At the twinkle of his piercing eye,
Life's deserts spring forth oceans from dry.
At the quake of his displeasure,
Crowning mountains fall to earth from a once tall measure.
At the stilling of his ease,
Comes forth the cool, the evening breeze.
Within the tower of his might,
Sinners turn from wrong to right.
In the pleasure of his calm is a holy, healing balm
(Jeremiah 8:22).[117]
Inspired by the fluttering of his angels' wings,
The meadowlark and all feathered creatures sing.

Sheltered beneath his protective roof,
My well-being and my health are proof
That in his envelope I am sealed,
And many once undiscovered sights,
sounds, and miracles
Are to the world, as a whole, revealed.

490. If one begins a project in doubt, one will end the project in failure.

491. Fishing takes patience. So does hooking your dreams (Matthew 10:22).[118]

492. It is only the body that gets buried in the ground, nothing else.

493. One is often influenced for the worse by intelligent beings invisible to one's eye.

494. To read a man's life one need only read the lines in his face.

495. Clothes dress the person; morality dresses the spirit.

496. One's dreams are meaningful journeys.

Love, when it is love, is …

Love Beyond the Physical

Love beyond the physical is love into the true,
Love so indivisible; love that's me, I found in you.
Love so incorruptible; love beyond all time.
Love for which I daily sought.
A love my gracious Lord made mine.
For in that soul that mirrors me, I saw you standing there,
Within my grasp, within my reach.
I saw us as the perfect pair.
Though touching what's perceived as real,
though stroking oft together,

When minds engage where soul's do meet,
the incline is forever.
The heart can feel what mind imagines;
the soul will glad receive
What flesh alone, though pressed together,
can never ev'r retrieve.
So when you seek a lover's touch,
be sure true love is there.
For if it's naught but physical,
what you thought you had will disappear.
The bed has rung, quite oft, sad note,
sung by two off-key.
They go from mate to mate to mate
for their blinded eyes refuse to see …
That love's beyond the physical;
'tis deep inside the true,
For what the other feels inside,
is felt inside of you.
That can't be touched by hands, by breasts,
by lips that are hard pressed,
But when your heart agrees with mine,
'tis true love at its best.
'Tis love beyond the physical and is every lover's quest.

497. Your future is malleable.

498. The more immensely we imagine, the bigger our infinity becomes.

499. Had enough yet?

500. Creative writing is a personal arrangement of existing thoughts and, sometimes, ideas, collected and reorganized to convey new ones.

Are there …
Children in Your Garden

With children in your garden, don't leave them to neglect
For they will grow up underfed
and have little self-respect.
They need sunshine, water, too; they need love and care.
With much encouragement you'll find
they can, in life, go anywhere.
Don't be afraid to hug them and tell them, "I love you."
'Cause if you don't, when they're grown up,
they'll never think of you.
The weeds and tares must oft be checked
to pull them from their minds.
There's no coincidence their yours, and this by God's design.
Children in your garden are nature's precious fruit,
Without them from God's Tree of Life
the world would be destitute (Revelation 22:2).[119]
Upon them rain your loving care,
shine on them love and trust,
And give them room for a few mistakes,
for healthy minds you must.
Probe their churning, silent minds,
awaken them to dream.
For things concrete are things first thought,
things thought more than they seem.
Don't plant them by the wayside,
where vultures dwell and prey,
Plant them deep within your heart,
and in your heart they'll stay.
Caress them and then smile and say,
"You're beautiful; you're sweet."
Encouragement will keep them from a life of self-defeat.
Children in your garden do never leave to chance.
Put all your best inside of them, and you, too, will advance.

A fruitful garden will emerge
in years, and when you're through,
Raising them the fruit they bear
will take good care of you.
The children in your garden, be to them forever true.

501. Life begins when it is seen as opportunity.

502. It is the love of fishing that makes even its difficulties enjoyable.

The Flower of April

April loves the flower,
The flower of its bloom.
April's sunshine showers
Its radiant perfume.
Its warmth and resurrection
Of things that were deceased,
The seasons now move forward
For the winter winds have ceased.

503. You're never too old.

504. Religious people without love in their hearts are like a supply house with no supplies.

505. The individual who figured he had time to complete many things in his life made the papers later that day because he ran out of it.

506. A writer collects from the environment meanings, spills them onto a piece of paper where there they are arranged in terms of his own life experience.

507. When one seeks with half a heart then one can only gain half a treasure.

508. The foreigner is only someone from another country, not another planet.

509. When the salesman said, "rust resistant," remember, he never said "rust proof."

510. With death comes amazement.

511. It's funny how people fear going to jail but do not fear going to hell.

512. If more people understood how important they already are, they wouldn't need so many "extra" things to make them feel that way.

513. As the man pleaded with his woman, "Honey, don't leave me; I'm a good man." whatever gave him the impression that she was looking for something good?

514. The fact that people pay attention to you does not make you more important than the people they don't.

515. The Lord put you in this world to add something to it.

516. How is it that intelligent people on the same planet allow other people on it to starve to death?

517. When your child strays from the path that is right, grab yourself a rod and lead him back (Proverbs 23:14).[120]

518. Jesus wrapped himself in the form of a man and came to earth as the Son of Man to demonstrate the possibilities of man.

519. When a soldier dies on the battlefield, his blood is required at the hands of those persons in government who sent him there.

520. Only a heart with God in it can hear the cries of the unborn.

521. Size and appearance are not even clues (1 Samuel 17:33, 41–42).[121]

522. If you have a tongue, speak your mind but only truth. If you have eyes to see, observe, but cast not thy gaze upon unholy things. If you have ears to hear, listen, but only to that which is good. If you have a mind to love, then don't mind loving everybody.

523. A heart that is close to God and utters its voice to him, is heard.

524. A man is born in debt to God.

525. In the Spanish language, the word *sin* is a preposition (or preposition) meaning, "on the outside of."

526. If this is your life, then tell death, "No!"

527. Remove the titles and the huge bank accounts, and their flesh is just as weak as yours.

528. If you let your desire wander, it will soon wander into mischief.

529. Looking for a crimeless society? Then seek eternal life in heaven through Jesus Christ.

530. Nothing well made is ever thrown together (Genesis 1:27).[122]

531. Love is so much easier to bear than hate.

532. Men and women involved in empty relationships have very little to say to one another.

533. Man fills his life with things that empty his life.(Proverbs 13:7).[123]

If it's filthy …
I'll Take a Mop

I'll take a mop and clean it up,
Earth's misery, its pain.
On blinded eyes I'd Windex spray
And wipe until no spot remained.
I'll take a sponge and sponge up grief,
And disinfect disease.
I'll scrub life from my power base
And cleanse this world just as I please.
I'll take a broom and sweep out sin,
The very cause that makes unclean,
That sends men dire consequence.

From their desperate hearts come things unseen.
But I'll take a mop; I'll clean it up.
That is, I only wish I could.
A mop called love would clean up things
And fill this world with so much good.
Let's take our mops and clean it up,
clean everything we should.

534. Pessimistic leaders are not leaders.

535. One's aura is painted by the color of one's mood.

What has caused the …
Birds' Jubilee

Why do birds have so much to say
In morning's way, at brink of day?
As dozens lark and tweet about,
Why do they sing, so loudly shout?
So I asked one bird,
"What jubilee has caused to sing your family?"
As he bounced away, he simply said,
"God's sun has just risen from the dead!"

536. Everything belongs to God.

537. Sports events were also immensely popular in ancient Rome, whose mighty empire came to a relatively speedy extinction.

The mysteries of God are not always evident …
Sign Concealed

Sign concealed and plain from view,
Depicts a soul unrisen;
In heart and mind and for the man,
To whom no "seal" is given (John 6:27; Revelation 9:4).[124]
The seal of God invites you to
A world unseen and also new.
The sign's concealed only to those
He says are not yet His' n.

538. A light bulb is a vacuumed container that houses a filament. When an electric current is passed through it, it houses a fiery filament. So, too, is the Christian who lets his light shine abroad that others might glorify God.

539. The more time you spend with a person, the better you get to know them. The same is true with God in prayer.

All too often more than one thing can be found inside …
The Present Wrapped

The present wrapped, so nicely, though,
and pretty ribbon tied,
Reminds me of a girl I knew
and hoped would be my bride.
But things fell through;
the woman only held my interest slight.
Our romance soared to mountains high
but dulled in similar passions night after night.
You see, it was the "package wrapped"

that keyed my interest so.
The mystery of her lovely contours
is what I wanted "unlocked" to know.
As a gift upon a birthday table
piques the question, "What
Lies beneath that shiny paper,
and its lovely bows and such?"
The mystery is what lies within,
and it's here I missed the point.
A birthday package and a human being
are things distinct and quite disjoint.
I "unwrapped" her package, seeking gifts
and treasures never known.
But what I found was emptiness
and treasures that were never shown.
The present wrapped was lovely, though,
and my eager eyes did never see
That package should be left alone
for it was never meant for me.
So many men tear open "gifts"
wrapped with love and so much care,
Seeking treasures there within
that vanish in thin air.
For the package cannot be the gift found only in the heart.
Love the woman, and you'll find true love
to be in life true art.
Leave that lovely package be
for before it is unwrapped,
The mystery that's within its soul
is what must first be tapped.
That lovely soul's a person first,
not an object to be used.
Never meant for careless fingers
and by careless hearts to be abused.

Such a lovely present wrapped
and tied with ribbons, lace, and strings.
Untouched, its simple beauty to
my soul brings gifts and treasured things.

540. A man rarely grows old where his thoughts do not.

541. Jail is a state (correctional institution) of mind, which is why those who end up in it do.

542. Time is a concern only for those who are running out of it.

543. Love is not passed on from heart to heart; it is passed on from God to each heart.

544. To be asleep is not always to be at rest (Hebrews 4:1).[125]

545. The adult is a product of his rearing ... of his choices ... but especially of his choices.

546. How much will a request to God generally cost you? At the least some kind of *change*.

547. Some of us without money are much richer than some of those who have lots of it.

548. When you share your love life with many different women, your love life is in pieces.

549. When people see themselves as less than others, they often have a strong dislike for those they feel themselves to be beneath.

550. It's not how pretty the person looks; it's how pretty the person feels.

551. A badge of authority does not shield a man from ... "what comes around" (Galatians 6:7).[126]

With a, "Ho, ho, ho!" my letter is …
Signed, Santa Claus

Santa Claus, the season bright doth ring your very name,
But sadly from the minds of youth
did you steal our Jesus Savior's fame.
For you don't really bear the gifts
for which the child of earth doth wait.
For you came from men's fantasies
and sparked the Christmas Day debate:
Is it Jesus or Saint Nicholas who bears the gift of love?
The one came from the North Pole,
and the other from above.
Which one does fill our stockings full
of peace and joy divine?
Which one hath said to only seek
and heaven you will find?
Which one to tell your children of,
which one for them to dream?
Who is this old St. Nicholas,
and what does "Santa" really mean?
"Ho, ho, ho! I came to steal the glory from the Lord!
For with their minds on only me,
the gift of Christ I've oft destroyed.
He was born the gift of love
to bring salvation's blessed key;
I was born to gather up his glory unto me!
I'm jolly old Saint Nicholas,
not what Christmas really means.
I came from men's fantasies;
I came from men's dreams.
I came in the Christmas night
to steal the glory of the Christmas Day.
It is me for whom the children wait;
it is I who steal their hope away.

Through me they'll never learn of how
God gave his only Son,
A gift for all humanity,
so that to his light they'd come.
Yes, he's the gift, eternal life,
he's knocking at the door,
But their hearts might never know of him,
if the news of him I can destroy!
It's me, St. jolly Nicholas, the title spells it plain.
Remove the n and place it last,
and Satan is my name!
With a ho, ho, ho I came to earth
to steal the news of Christ,
So that little minds might leave him out
from year to year their life.
They look to me to bring them gifts,
but in truth, I steal away
The blessed birth of Jesus Christ,
and thus I steal his blessed way (John 14:6).[127]
I am the thief of Christmastime,
and Santa is my name.
In the nighttime of men's ignorance,
I come and steal the Savior's fame.
To erase from earth Christ's blessed name
for this to earth I came."
Signed, Santa Claus.

552. The man who refuses to love ends up with some very serious heart *dis-ease* problems … really.

553. Some people say, "When it's your time to go, it's your time to go.", never thinking once that a man's life could be more profitable to God and lengthened (Matthew. 21:19).[128]

554. Material wealth makes you rich by the world's standards. Love makes you rich by God's standards.

555. The man who thinks that he can handle a poisonous serpent will soon lie dead next to it.

556. Some things, just like people, don't belong together.

557. Salvation is the envelope; you are its contents. Jesus's blood is the postage, as in "already paid."

This Day Blessed

This day, blessed, life's haven revealed.
Sweet words are unfolded; the book now unsealed
(Revelation 5:1; Isaiah 29:11).[129]
Thoughts are enlightened; my eyes plain perceive
That life is all blessed when we somehow believe.
Believe all can happen, that miracles can be,
That blindness is doubt, but faith, eyes that see.
That see all is beauty, and see all is blessed;
That see God provides all that is best.
That see in employing God's heavenly law,
His invitation's to you from his fountain to draw.
This day is blessed; look around, and you'll see
God's blessed salvation enter in and be free!
"This day is blessed," cries the height and the deep,
Cries all vegetable things and all things that creep;
Cries the insect, his kingdom, cries the hill and the shore.
Were the rocks to cry out, they'd cry all the more.
Proclaims all things living, that is, except man,
Who has the power of reason, and his thoughts to expand.
The least understanding of all creatures that be,
And none are more backward, more backward than he!
How could he not see all the good the Lord brings?

Does not understand why the meadowlark sings.
Refusal, refusal, his keynote reply,
And when things fall apart, his response always, "Why?"
Look unto the hills from whence cometh your power.
Perceive God brings life with each earthly shower!
Be still, oh man, know that the Husbandman cares.
Behold all the wonderful things that he shares:
The sunshine, the flowers; the warmth, and the breeze;
Earth's natural landscape that he dresses with ease!
Grain in abundance, and meat for our needs.
He feeds you, oh blind man, seems to this you'd concede.
The farmer, the doctor, the skilled craftsman, too.
Stop a minute; pay attention
to the things God brings to you.
· The tailor; the fishermen who harvests the seas.
And the sweetness of honey he brings from the bees!
The engineer, those in science, who create and invent,
The abundance of talents, declaring, "All men are sent!"
The list is too long to incorporate here,
But my plea is to you all on earth and sincere.
Wake up, and see thee that glory surrounds.
Remember the quail and the manna sent down (Exodus 16:15).[130]
Add reason to rhyme: one plus one equals two;
Realize all the benefits sent daily to you!
And soon you will utter as your song's oft refrain,
That this day is blessed when I do life retain.
This day is blessed, and I'm blessed in this day,
Forever in Jesus's truth, life, and his way!

558.   Children's minds are molded by the fingers of their eyes and ears.

559.   Man is a race of immortals, for the souls of men never die.

I'll be quiet and still …
At Least for Now

At least for now I think I will,
At least for now be still.
And if the time has come, arrived,
At least by now I've tried.
At least in time, in time I know,
Where in Christ I go.
At least for now I think I will,
In law and truth be still.

560. The man many times said, "I love you," to the maid, and once he got what he wanted from her, he never said it again.

561. Each day has its own work.

562. Take all of your questions to Jesus. Leave them there, and they will soon dissolve into answers.

If they could, they would tell you …
Don't Come to This Place

In the thick, dark abyss … pain.
Torture so senseless, it appears insane,
It's agony not yet reported but is written on every face.
If they could come back and tell you,
They'd say, "Don't come to this place!"
The Devil and his angels; you thought Hitler was bad.
You'd think the worst of human torture was a vacation pass.
You'd think the worst earthly misery
Was a beauty beyond time and space,
If you could hear the lost souls crying,

"Don't come to this place!"
Pain after pain, with no shutdown day or night;
No possibility of any ease, or of end, or of flight.
Ungodly torture as Satan keeps up its pace.
All lost cry to their families, "Don't come to this place!"
A low-grinding misery, or people gasping for air;
Bodies ripped limb from limb, and their still
living parts flung everywhere.
With pain always attached to each soul,
punishment is forever the case.
If you could read their thoughts, they're thinking,
Don't come to this place!
Opening upon opening belches fire and ash.
Weeping and wailing with each merciless lash
From their tormentor's whips that with barbed wire is laced,
Their flesh always torn, they cry,
"Don't come to this place!"
Terrifying creatures whose teeth are as unrelenting nails
Seals the lost soul's flesh, its fate,
from hell's unrelenting jails.
You could run, but those demons just enjoy the chase …
You would wish every moment
you hadn't come to this place.
Imagine yourself baked in an oven
at four thousand degrees,
And the oven door remaining locked,
regardless of your pleas.
As hopeless tears filled your eyes,
and terror filled your face,
Wouldn't you want to tell your loved ones,
"Don't come to this place!"
In everlasting terror you'd be destined ever to remain;
You would never leave there, and never would the pain.
Suffering would always fill your soul,
and great fear you would always taste

As you scream for anyone who might hear,
"Don't come to this place!"
Can you imagine being buried alive,
remaining awake and never found,
Retaining all your consciousness
while little worms ate your flesh beneath the ground?
You, confined, unable to move,
for your sinful life had sealed your fate.
Don't even try it; I know you'd be shouting to others,
"Don't come to this place!"
Countless others there in an oceanic barbecue—
Doctors, celebrities, also the poor,
and those who posed as preachers, too—
Billions upon billions who rejected God's grace
Are now howling and shrieking,
"Don't come to this place!"
And remember, it's still the seeds you've sown,
all the company makes no difference,
For in hell each man's pain is his own.
Religions, traditions, ancient practices
you thought to be true,
You thought would bring eternal life and eternal joy, too;
Yellow, black, red, or white,
earth's every quarter, from every race. Their sad refrain in unison is,
"Don't come to this place!"
Whoremongers and the abominable
are no different than you
For if you doubt God in the least,
you'll be cast in hell, too.
If the righteous scarcely make it in,
though you think you're a religious ace,
Just by exalting yourself as such,
you're on your way to that awful place.
So to all who are in doubt
and think that hell is here on earth,

I warn you, this is just a picnic
if you deny our God's new birth.
Lost souls you can't hear screaming
for they've disappeared without a trace.
But to some their screams are quite audible
as they cry to all,
"Don't come to this place!"

563. Things have changed. God has not.

564. A mother once said, "I love my child; that's why I don't beat him." One day, when the child was big enough and strong enough, he beat the mother. I wonder what his reason was?

565. Who tangled the web?

566. To man, Satan promises many things. Man in his quest to gain them, partakes of the many forbidden fruits offered (Genesis 3:1–6).[131]

567. A bullet once fired from a gun is a committed thing.

568. People who are looking for happiness in this life ought to fill their lives with doing for others, and they will find it.

569. A thief is the one standing in a crowd with very still hands but incessantly rapid eye movement.

570. When you stand before the Lord in judgment, two things will matter: everything you did while here on earth and everything you didn't do.

571. A man's craving for recognition reflects an impoverished self-esteem.

572. Ideas are the materials from which our tomorrows are built.

573. People, like cars, are not run down by years but by lack of maintenance.

574. Some gifts are given from the hands, others from the heart.

575. A house left unattended will deteriorate. The same holds true for one's conduct.

576. No matter what it is down here, it ain't nothin like up there!

577. One can only learn as much as he or she accepts in the way of instruction.

578. This life and the world through which we travel are merely an exercise (Hebrews 12:11).[132]

579. Your soul never dies.

580. Time spent in prison halts the progress of time.

581. Sometimes big things start with little things.

582. So many seek their identities in things outside of who they really are.

As our day draws to a close we witness the …

Splendor of the Evening Graces

Splendor of the evening graces,
yielding to the dusking tide,
Shadows prepare for tomorrow
those who'll see the other side.
For evening draws us on forever
to the things that might to be.
We know not if we'll see tomorrow
for life's future is its mystery.
The golden sun is disappearing,
melting into shades of night;
Fading light grows on more distant
as it travels far away in flight.
Shadows cover earth and deeply,
but wait, appears the evening star
To give us hope that God is near us
and that his love is never far.

583. Some individuals feel that the higher they move up the ladder of success, the more people they can look down on.

584. Many parents would rather *tell* the child what to do; only a select few are willing to *show* them what to do.

585. Foundless suspicion is too weighty for love.

586. People who make a spectacle of themselves in public were probably not given enough attention as children.

587. We have the convenience of the supermarket because of the farmer. Have you thanked God for him today?

588. Discuss the problem, and you may come up with a solution. Discuss solutions to solving the problem, and you instantly begin the process of eliminating the problem.

589. In the military, a man does not hold a rank; it is the rank that holds the man.

590. Speed as an action can be either diligence or haste.

591. When lust seeks to strangle a man's heart, shame intervenes, delivering him from his sinful and burning passion, cooling its flames, and turning his heart about.

592. Pain in your life? Are you listening?

593. Every man is born with at least one talent (Matthew 25:14, 15).[133]

594. Detergent for the dirty clothes; the blood of Jesus for the dirty soul.

595. When a man is satisfied, a smile often dresses his face.

596. The monkey, when asked, "Are you happy in your cage?" answered by eating his free banana.

597. If you are down, when you have a friend, you are never out.

598. Very little can be hidden from the eyes of a wise man.

599. Many possibilities lie atop the surface of a blank piece of paper.

If they saw themselves as they really are …
They Would Be Ashamed

They would be ashamed if they only knew
That their lives were full of sin, the sins they daily do.
They would be ashamed of all the time they spent unwise,
As but a form of godliness in a hypocrite's disguise
(2 Timothy 3:5).[134]
They would be ashamed to tell the secrets in their hearts
And how their minds did many times
from righteousness depart.
How their thoughts did daily
with their neighbors' spouses lay.
How they never thought of God
and how they never stopped to pray.
They would be ashamed
for unfit words they oft have spoken,
Thinking righteousness irrelevant,
"It's only God's law that I've broken."
They would be ashamed that Sundays
were for watching sports
Or washing cars, no godly things;
what a sad report!
They would be ashamed to find
that hell, the place, is real,
And the sinner's fate to be their own
when judgment is revealed.
They would be ashamed, my friend,
if they only knew
All the things they must prepare,
all the things they have to do.
They would be ashamed
because they never sacrificed,
Never thinking God is real,
never *gave* their lives to Christ.

They would be ashamed
and only wished that they could tell
All the unashamed that they are burning
day and night in hell (Mark 9:43).[135]
They would be ashamed. They would be ashamed.

600. A thief is satisfied only with stealing.

601. You told her you loved her, but you could have *shown* her the same thing with flowers.

602. When tomorrow is the same as today, it's not really tomorrow.

Peace is …
Inside, Within

The moon and the stars lie within me,
The mountains and purplish peaks.
When I close my eyes, I imagine
For the vision of God is for him who will seek.
The sea and its shore meet inside me,
They are balanced by God in between.
So that when there's a need,
Just tuck you inside you
For all things lie within
where no season is lean.

603. An honest nickel carries more weight than a dishonest dollar.

604. A lofty dream caught up in the heavens of one's desire is brought down to earth by hard work (Ecclesiastes 5:3).[136]

605. The man who steals takes … (the name of the Lord his God in vain) (Proverbs 30:9).[137]

606. A man without God in his heart is just dust with a soul.

607. Doubt distrusts what it cannot see.

608. Saying a thing is sometimes a precursor to doing a thing, as in, "I'm gonna kill you."

609. If children present little problems when they are small, guess what happens as they grow older.

610. Talking to a child teaches him the art of verbal communication. The occasional use of the rod teaches him the art of understanding (Proverbs 23:13–14).[138]

611. Without self-confidence, what you wear still doesn't look that good on you.

612. The human spirit soars above its oppression when it dreams!

613. Money might buy you a mansion on a hill, but not peace of mind to live comfortably in it.

614. A building with no windows is a building with no sunshine.

By faith and trust my wife …
Tina Made It Through

You made it through the storm,
Through the tempest, through the rain.
Thank God we'll never wonder
If we'll see your face again.
Only Jesus understands
the trial that you've come through.
No one but him and other souls
That passed that same way, too.
You've carried a tremendous load,

Your cross you had to bear,
And because you did,
In life you will be stronger everywhere.
You made it through the element;
You made it through the storm.
Your journey for our Lord and Christ
Most surely will go on.

615. In the process of making your cake, did you leave any of the main ingredient out?

616. While there are many people in the world who are starving to death, there are other people in the world who are gambling their money away, calling it fun.

617. What a man thinks about will be one day what he is not just thinking about (Proverbs 23:7).[139]

The swe-e-e-t apple of ...

Sin

S-s-s-s-sin is the Serpent's hiss
That cons you but to think it bliss.
It coils in a place unknown,
Its fluid poison and fangs unshown.
Its voice with melody appears,
An innocent apple crying, "Bite me here!"
Though you were told to do so not,
In sin's web of intrigue, you are now intertwined;
you are caught.
By the softest words the Serpent did you assail
Till it never dawned on you,
you were locked in sin's jail!

Till the spoiled bread and the bitter drink
'Cause now your heart within to think:
I've been beguiled this time again,
To fail the things I did amend.
The s-s-s-s-sting of the Serpent's hiss did bite,
And in it I found pure delight,
To oft indulge in pleasures vain,
To strengthen o'er me the Devil's reign.
I'd forgotten the Serpent, subtle and wise,
The master of darkness and the father of lies
(2 Corinthians 11:14).[140]
Yes, s-s-s-s-s-sin has a hiss,
But its rattle you won't hear,
Designed by the Devil so you won't know him near
Till he strikes with the venomous poison of sin,
Ensuring the death of your life now begin.
The choice is but yours to watch as you pray
(Matthew 26:41).[141]
To maintain life's vigil along its perilous way.
That s-s-s-s-s-sin is the Serpent's tackle and lure,
That will land you in hell forever for sure.

618. Vision paints a future not yet visible to the naked eye.

619. Fear is the absence of faith. Love is the absence of fear (1 John 4:18).[142]

There's little doubt …
I've Seen You Before

I've seen you before, and what is my name?
And who would I conquer? What soul would I claim?

And who is among you my rage he'll disdain?
I've seen you before. My name is cocaine.
I've seen you, the low class, in ghetto towns, too;
I've seen you, the middle class,
but I'm not quite through.
I've measured you uptown, your stature, your fame;
Are you better than me? My name is cocaine.
I've taken you down from position and power.
I've robbed you of guilt and of shame and desire.
I've taken your will; you're not quite the same ...
I won you, my child, my name is cocaine.
When you were a thriving, intelligent being,
I saw you beyond the self you were seeing.
I figured you out for I saw weakness there.
You did not take heed when your friends said beware.
Though you were not looking, the danger was plain.
I slip-trapped you into my world called cocaine.
You reasoned within you that your soul couldn't be bought,
When really the truth was it was me that you sought.
So now that you've found me, it is you who's to blame.
You're now a statistic in the world of cocaine.
I can buy you and sell you; I can cause you to steal.
I can make you turn tricks for I've frozen your will.
I have brought you so low till you have no more shame,
What did it to you, my brother? Cocaine!
You heard others say I was an excellent high.
You reasoned, "No harm, if just a little I try."
"A little ... of me? (*chuckle*) temporarily insane.
You play with the Devil when you play with cocaine.
I've seen you before whether white collar or blue,
Whether doctor or lawyer, I don't care what you do.
I'll reduce you to bones wrapped in skin, just a frame.
Just a living-dead person who tried out cocaine.
There were many who warned you; you were already told
I'd reduce once-held youth to something wrinkled and old.

Ambition, desire, I am able to drain.
I've seen you before; my name is cocaine.
So let me now bid you a final farewell
And warn of the horrible story I tell.
I'll take you before you die into hell,
And you'll learn of my fame for I am cocaine.

620. Like a helium-filled balloon, the lighter one's thoughts, the higher he or she rises above a world of troubles.

621. When a character in a motion picture shoots or stabs another person, it is the *idea* portrayed on the screen that is dangerous in the mind of a child.

622. Worldliness fills one with emptiness.

623. A little love nourishes a healthy tomorrow.

624. It is said that the sun makes things grow … and it does.

625. Satan's job is to try, to tempt, and to test.

626. If it does not fit and you try to wear it, it still won't fit.

627. If you say to your children, "I love you," they will probably believe it.

628. Monday through Sunday are just names we give each day of the week, but what difference does the day make if you do the same worthless things all week long?

629. If man can't walk on water, why then did Jesus demonstrate to the world that it was possible?

630. Thank me for what I do for you, and I'll probably do more. God may feel the same way.

631. You can't teach what you don't live.

632. The blind in our society have trouble seeing … past skin color.

633. Education also means the power to educate.

634. Satan, in fishing for men, baits his hook with those things that they desire.

635. When a man's heart is close to God he can trust the things imagined.

636. Truth is most threatening to the enemies of truth.

637. Never let a small child out of your sight.

638. Within a man's heart lie all his possibilities.

639. Many on earth think that money equals happiness. Many who have lots of it know that's not true.

640. In its capacity and eagerness to express itself, man's tongue has often unintentionally lied (James 3:2).[143]

641. Failure is the absence of success. Success is the absence of a mind to fail.

642. A request made by man to God is often accompanied by a request made by God to man.

643. Those who champion the cause of the oppressed become the target of those who do not.

644. Love is a peaceful giant.

645. Cheerfulness is a fruitful field that refreshes the weary traveler.

646. What is life without joy? It is not life.

647. When one soldier falls, the cause doesn't.

648. Confidence is a strong city.

649. A small child … clay.

650. All the things that a man thinks he is satisfying by greed he is actually starving.

651. The more man advances, the less concerned he seems to be with the God that allows him to.

652. Ugly is not how a person looks. Ugly is how a person thinks … or how a person feels …or what a person does.

Remember Me

Remember me
As thee thou sit on throne of grace,
Though thief I be from child art were,
And stolen gifts with sacrifices gave I not never.
Be that I from separated life to death be doom.
I did you not tarry with.
Lord, but me remember.
Cleanse when I self to cling in thee with.
Gone us we in death to life.
Thy paradise in now forever when
Said thou us to this:
Thou will today
With me in be
Eternal I in life in thee.

653. When you arrive at a certain "place" in your life, you have not traveled the distance in feet or in inches.

654. The difference between now and fifty years ago has little to do with automation technology.

655. Information whose basis is truth is called knowledge. Information whose basis is falsehood is called garbage.

656. If your life can be bought for cheap, there is very little of value in it.

I decided to share with you …

A Thought or Two

I'll share with you a thought or two,
a word, or phrase without a clue.
I'll carry time, it, to and fro

and anywhere I choose to go.
For when I write I can become
of the things I think, the total sum.
A phrase with no idea in sight
has taken wing and been given flight.
Piercing, dip, and swoop and glide;
come along with me on a path untried!
Behold what lasting things prevail,
A truth that cannot never fail.
For what you see and do accept
is what inside your heart is kept
And if not fit of good to stay,
will rot your poor soul fast away.
Think only good; you'll find in time
that your feelings are as good as mine.
Tap the wealth that's found within.
Oh lonely soul, it's time … begin!
Wisdom falls to earth like rain
Whose truth can only God explain.
For but a simple thought or two
will open doors your whole life through.
A phrase with no idea in sight
has taken wing and been given flight.
With ideas that pierce the world's domain,
The mighty pen will victory on earth retain!

657. Are you aware that God answers prayer?

658. What's in your heart is what you are.

659. Never strike agreements with an enemy.

660. Of the modern-day computer: how can any machine be more extraordinary than the mind from which its design emerged?

661. You are guilty of more than you think.

A historic and very tragic incident in Philadelphia history …

On the Move

Skies are graying overhead; as time goes on, we count the dead …
Our neighborhood in ruins lies; for what did the movers die?
They sift the rubble, bit by bit, to see what pieces just might fit
The puzzle of "Black Monday's" doom that did eleven lives consume.
As controversies storm about, they who point the finger shout,
"Why did you drop the bomb!" They cry,
"Why did you drop the bomb?"
If I could perceive a way to clarify that fateful day,
a day wherein we did behold the dooming tale destruction told.
Our mouths hung open in silent despair
as our lives through thick smoke vanished to nothing in thin air.
We count our loss, 'tis gone away, will ne'er return, 'tis gone away.
Who thought their end would ever be a future no one here could see?
And that their final ending fame would perish in an unjust flame.
Who'd not flee the fire's fear that rendered them no longer here?
Bullet fragments in charred remains? Testify and make it plain
That child, adult, make no mistake, from
the fearsome blaze had no escape.
They who did that day depart still wound the spared and living hearts.
Of we who loved, of we who cared, whose
grief not in the least was spared.
The movers, radical their shift, no longer here their shouts to lift,
Were on the move to God knows where, only
God knows what they now declare.
Skies are graying overhead; as time goes on, we count the dead …
Our neighborhood in ruins lie; for what did the movers die
(Glossary Entry, May 13, 1985)?[144]

662. What we have is not always what we keep. What we keep is not always what we have.

663. A certain man sat down at his table to eat a meal. He did not bow his head or ask God to bless his food. Sometime later, after his near fatal bout with food poisoning, the same man had occasion to once again sit down at that same table to eat a meal. He still did not bow his head and ask God to bless his food.

664. When you talk to God, which is prayer, then you learn to discern his voice when he talks to you (John 10:3–5).[145]

665. Fear is the absence of love (1 John 4:18).[146]

666. A dream of the head upon one's bed is more than just a dream of the head (Daniel 4:5).[147]

667. Love is more powerful than thoughts.

668. We all have one Father.

669. An opinion is a judgment (Matthew 7:1).[148]

670. If always means forever, then what is the meaning of eternal damnation?

671. He was a connoisseur of women. Notice, I said, "He *was*."

672. If visible things come from invisible things (e.g., solid matter from things not seen, such as atoms and protons), then it stands to reason that matter is just a denser form of the unseen, which is spirit.

Where lives are wasting away …

The Corner Gathers

The corner gathers aimless hearts, the riffraff and the blue.
The corner gathers our young men; has the corner gathered you?
The corner gathers empty hands with nothing much in sight.
The corner gathers darkness there for it fears to gather light.
The corner gathers broken hearts whose esteem cannot be found;
The corner says, "Come lay on me, with your faces to the ground!"
Its aim: "Imprison bright young minds, intelligent to be.

Destroy their sight, their vision for the blind can never see."
The corner are the few that watch, the few that be in power
Who destroy the hope of youthful minds and the masses they devour,
Ensuring they remain cast down, their will to never raise,
Destitute and fruitless all their earthly days.
Our youth, the strong, are hanging on the corners of the street,
Having bowed themselves to failure and to loss and self-defeat.
But no matter what it seems, you must remember all the time,
All's not lost for God has said,
"Behold, all souls are mine" (Ezekiel 18:4).[149]

673. Life wants to go on.

674. Christians are known by the things they do. Christians are known by the things they don't do.

675. A man's future is held in his destiny. A man's destiny is held in his future. A man's destiny is also revealed in his future at the same time it is held there. But, his destiny is also held in his present. A man's present and future are one and the same. What, however, a man is destined to be, if not predestined by God can be altered by his individual choices.

676. True Christian character is measured by the strain of human interaction.

677. Greed only leaves one hungry.

Retrieve

Retrieve, retrieve, just bring it back.
Return to me, oh thou,
For thee it is will "trieve" me so,
And to thee it is I bow.

Turn me to thy way of light.
Cleanse my will, my soul;
Save me from my fractured being.
Make me sane, me whole.
Retrieve, retrieve, just bring me back
To life, to love, to thee.
Return my spirit on high, oh Christ,
Till sanctified it be.

678. Cast not thoughtful desire upon that which is thy neighbor's (Exodus 20:17).[150]

679. Jesus has a different approach to the sinner; it's called love.

680. As shoes to the feet and an overcoat to one's back, so is confidence to the soul.

681. What we deserved was death. What we received was mercy (John 3:16).[151]

682. Lord, thou art all right!

683. When is it too late (Luke 12:20)?[152]

684. Failure belongs only to those who quit trying.

685. If they are willing to legislate laws to kill the unborn and to assist in suicide, what's next?

686. It stands to reason that the Devil would refer to a dog and not to God as man's best friend. To understand why, just spell the word "dog" backward!

687. The term "half-baked" means that you did not wait long enough on God.

688. When applied to a vain person, flattery will get you everywhere.

689. God took away a certain man's eyesight to help him *see* better.

690. Behind the aged face, too often does not lie aged wisdom.

691. Someone who flirts with death is not far from it.

692. Unmanaged anger ... destruction (Psalm 37:8).[153]

693. Plant a seed ... nurture it ... watch it grow.

694. Government is a mechanism for managing the conduct of its nation's citizens. It is also the mechanism for the management and concise operation of that nation's business affairs. Now, "the system" is how, exactly, that mechanism is handled.

695. A woman's true beauty is not always that which can be seen with the eyes (Proverbs 31:10).[154]

696. Replace doubt with faith.

697. The average adult is one who has unlearned the ability to believe.

698. The child who dismembers a doll is telling the world how they see themselves.

699. What did you do today?

700. How can anything material or physical satisfy emotional emptiness?

701. No cloudy day is permanent.

702. He who takes his own life takes hell into his bosom.

703. Repetition reinforces learning (Psalm 119:15).[155]

704. Those who fail can always try. Those who try are never failures.

705. In sports, teamwork is, in essence, the one body at work to save itself from defeat.

706. Jesus is our lifeline.

707. Satan knows his own.

708. The man who believes not cannot be made to believe what he believes not.

709. When the heart is attacked, it sometimes means that Christ was not there to defend it (Revelation 3:20).[156]

710. Time lasts only as long as your stay on this earth.

711. In terms of race, what color is an idea?

712.   Real pain begins with the death of a lost soul.

Beloved

Beloved and sanctified thou art.
Your meanings dwell within the heart;
Tis hidden thy expanse unknown,
Unshown to me, unshown.
Wake'd thou by interrupted sleep,
a price to pay, my vow to keep,
And promised to thy soul on high,
The Word, his truth, one can't deny.
A thought, its visit, did come my way.
I pondered it that very day.
Though it seemed displaced from time,
Its meaning was forever mine.
It taught its lesson well to me,
Undressed itself, its mystery,
Imparting an eternal rest
from years of life's enduring test.
I part my way tis to the end,
and to my soul did life extend.
A meaning not in words was told,
More pure to me than gold.
More pure to me than fuller's white (Mark 9:3),[157]
More grand than life's most grand delight.
More satisfying to my soul
than anything my heart could hold.
Its height more statuesque than time;
its meaning one cannot define.
Its fathomed deep not understood,
Of all the things that mankind should.
Beloved and sanctified thou art,

> I know ye shan't not ever part.
> The knowledge of you always brings
> Life's meaningful and lasting things.

713. Jesus: the Word. The answer. The Savior.

714. There are many accepted religious forms of belief along with their texts that refer to the Bible. Why is it then that the Bible has no need to refer to them?

715. What good is a tool in the hands of one not skilled in its use?

716. An open mind easily opens up to good ideas.

717. Experience, though it cannot be physically contained or packaged, is carried with you everywhere you go.

718. Love is not the body; it's the soul.

719. If you could tell truly what you love on this earth, it would seldom be yourself.

720. Faith is uncompromised knowing.

721. Sin has a cure (Jeremiah 8:22).[158]

722. Take a big job, divide it into parts, and you divide its bigness.

723. It is not the color of the skin that matters but the color of the heart.

724. A person is made of what they believe.

725. You will pay for everyone of your choices.

726. Death rarely announces its coming.

727. Love is only hard when you don't want to.

728. Those who willfully harm others always end up in the land of "what comes around" (Galatians 6:7).[159]

729. Pay your bills.

730. People who want to be accepted by others into a particular social arena often pay a very high price for admission.

731. A person's "fate" changes with his or her choices.

732. If I love you, it shows, and the things that commonly follow love do not have to be extracted by request.

733. Love makes two things one.

734. To sum up one's life is to tally all the good that one has done in it.

735. Sad but true: Man-made computers make more use of their memory than man himself does.

736. Tomorrow is today.

737. Man may make things, but has created nothing.

738. Do you have a life insurance policy? If you haven't given your *Whole Life* to Jesus Christ, you don't.

739. A tree's age is told by its annual rings. A man's age is told by the lines in his face.

740. A man is misled only when his desire is.

741. Three quarters of the earth's surface is water. Three quarters of a man's body is water. The earth is man in macrocosm. Man is the earth in microcosm.

742. The man who rises early in the morning is in a position to get things done.

743. The tears that flow now from a child's eyes due to necessary discipline will cut short the inevitable rivers of tears that will flow throughout his life (and yours) due to the absence of that discipline (Proverbs 23:14).[160]

744. To the aspiring author: the story is quite capable of writing itself!

745. A profane tongue immerses one's entire being in filth.

746. One of the things you cannot take from a man are his choices.

747. Right, as a flag flown in turbulence, continues to stand.

748. When death is seen doubtlessly approaching, man's understanding of an impending judgment is not only made clear to him, but certain!

749. A tropical storm showers trillions of raindrops; each one individual, each one contributory.

750. Forgiveness purges the soul.

751. Is the grass greener, or …?
No matter how physically attractive she is, men tend to tire from the sameness of one woman. As their imaginations drift out over a sea of countless women, the invisible riptide of that which is imagined tows them into the abyss of thoughtless desire. Upon waking, a man finds from that illicit bed two empty souls that have been introduced to one another and have parted ways more empty than when they met.

752. All that one possesses, he or she only seems to.

753. The better wine comes with the aging process. What of the better man?

754. Standard in the courtroom is the argument, which must be supported by the evidence. The evidence is then examined by the jury (or judge) who is charged with rendering a verdict. Here, however, several problems arise. Has vital evidence been withheld from the jury (suppressed)? Or has as an electrifying performance by way of charismatic persuasion displaced the reason and judgment of the jury? And where does justice lie when an innocent man has been falsely convicted of a crime he did not commit?

755. Directing one's attention to God, whether in prayer or in rejoicing, is a form of praise.

756. As the gates of a man's life close behind him what comes next either opens up to embrace him, or, swallows him alive!

757. What's behind door number three? Don't let your life be a guessing game.

I found …
Something Sweet

Something sweet, something kind, something pure, something true;
Something real, something sound, something great; something for you.
Something always, something reliable, something
outstanding, something stable;
Something there when I'm down that will not leave; something able.
Something now, something full, something happened when we met;
Something supplying what I need and hasn't stopped supplying yet.
Something grand, something sure, something deep inside my heart;
Something there by my side that forges life into life's art.
Something willing, something constant, a
thing more valuable than gold;
Something there not just today but for men since times of old.
Something mellow, something lavish, a thing
of wonder, something sweet;
The man whose called our Lord and Savior
whom I wish the world to meet!

758. Even the very wise must wait on wisdom.

759. Now divides time in half.

760. The preacher from the pulpit utters his mind, his beliefs, his thoughts, and sometimes things that don't even exist within him.

761. The fall breaks forth into astonishing color, pageantry, and beauty. So, too, in the *fall* of evil men (Proverbs 29:2).[161]

762. Man's might, might. God's might will!

763. Hang-ups are hung up in the mind.

764. Women are like a school of fish for the man with a strong line, seeking to hook one of them.

765. Though a man capture all the worlds prizes yet will his soul be empty of the one thing the world cannot give him … eternal life through Christ Jesus.

766. As the base runner slid across home plate, attempting to beat the throw that arrived at the same time he did, the umpire, crying out, made his call …! The soul is the base runner. The throw is from Satan. The umpire is God. Even in the game of baseball, the umpire might, through human error, declare a runner, "Safe!", when, in all truth, he was beaten by the throw. So, too, in the game of life. Sometimes when someone has been truly thrown out by Satan (justly accused of sin), God can declare him, "Safe!" by the redemptive blood of Christ.

767. An individual one day found himself and discovered a person he had never met.

768. Young children need their sleep.

769. The embryo is an individual.

770. Some people want to be famous but don't know why.

771. In the bowels of the earth lie active seas of fire and ash (Revelation 19:20).[162]

772. Why would a loving God give you everything you want?

773. Adolf Hitler was a vessel of complete hate.

774. What one looks for one always finds.

775. God gave you life. Now you have to give him something back!

776. For what reason do men still hate Jesus (John 7:7)?[163]

777. Only when you take your eyes off of the water can you walk on it (Matthew 14:30–31).[164]

778. We are given a very short life to accomplish as much good in it as we can.

779. Sample some things in life, and you may not live to sample others.

780. Murder by consent is no less the crime.

781. If thoughts come from the mind, where do ideas come from?

782. What I learned for myself I taught to others.

783. No one on earth, no matter how strong or influential, can stop a hurricane. So the most powerful people on earth aren't.

784. A lie is accepted as truth only by a liar.

785. The sea is another world. To "see" is another world.

786. Hatred ruins the heart.

787. The mighty of the earth only think they are.

788. At Hiroshima and Nagasaki the war ended ... only for some.

789. God will never forget what you said to him in prayer.

790. Most poor people pick the poorest topics to talk about.

791. You don't have to plant a million seeds, only one, and eventually that one seed will feed a million people.

792. To get an almost impossible job done, all you have to do is begin somewhere!

793. When a person does not like you, the reasons are many; the reasons are any.

794. To know what the foreigner wants out of life, just think about the things you want out of life.

795. Leadership propels ideas.

796. Man's hidden agenda: lust.

797. The flesh is sweet ... for now.

798. To the rich and powerful, other human beings are just chess pieces on a game board.

799. The man who possesses only the things that can be taken away from him may be wealthy but can never be rich (Matthew 6:19–21).[165]

800. Gravity pulls ... so does negative thinking, and though they both pull downward, there is nothing negative about gravity.

801. When there is no balance in a relationship between a man and a woman, the one is always looking for more than the other has to offer.

802. Even if you think you have a reason to hate someone, you still don't have a good one.

803. That which is pursued must be first dreamt.

804. Why lose everything (Matthew 16:26)?[166]

805. God's army … Behold what power (Psalm 82:6).[167]

806. If one proves a point before others, a lying heart will still not accept that proof.

807. Cold revenge is not as satisfying a meal as forgiveness.

808. The mind retains as crystal-clear images all of life's experiences, which include everything it has come in contact with, whether seen, tasted, touched, or felt emotionally.

809. All truth will be known in the hereafter.

810. Simple math: a faithful husband plus a faithful wife equals all the good things that marriage has to offer.

811. A man in love with fishing is in love with more than the catching of fish.

812. The answer that you are looking for is not always the answer that you are looking for.

813. The convinced, no matter what is shown them, are hardly persuaded.

814. Whatever it is, God can erase it.|

815. In most courtrooms, the spoils go to the most convincing argument, not the evidence.

Anything can be accomplished, but …
It Starts with an Idea

It starts with an idea, with a thought in your head;
Not with something you heard or just something you said.
It starts when you tap that hidden mystery inside,
The all-knowing presence that is master and guide.
It starts with desire held deep within;
A churning thought process where all things begin.
It starts with an idea, and where it travels will be
All the things in your heart that you just thought could be.

816. Discouragement drains a man of his possibilities.

817. Gifts are given by God. Their use here on earth is determined by the recipient.

818. It does not matter whether you believe there's a God or not, judgment is still coming.

819. If a thought comes into your mind you think important and useful, don't take a chance on losing it; write it down!

820. The masses can never be controlled by the mighty few (Mark 12:12).[168]

821. Each time you prepare to satisfy your hunger with bread made available to you that day, remember to do something for the world's hungry.

822. In … sight (Luke 17:21).[169]

823. What lust craves it will never satisfy.

824. You may not be able to bless your own food, but God will if you ask him.

825. The true riches are very hard to get your *hands* on.

826. Unnatural affection points to a damaged childhood.

827. If it's broke, don't complain about who broke it.

828. The mind, like our nation, has many states.

829. For the man close enough, God is power on tap (1 Kings 18:36–38).[170]

830. The destruction of the temple fostered its resurrection (John 2:19).[171]

831. Somewhere in your future lies your eternity.

832. Between birthdays there may not be another one.

833. Nothing with a soul comes to an end.

834. No sowing … no reaping.

835. From within a seed, by way of its demise, emerges its resurrected body!

836. The lonely elderly need a friend called Jesus.

837. If you can't see it, how do you know it's there (Hebrews 11:1)?[172]

838. A friend has your back. He who is not a friend will put a knife in it!

839. One who distrusts everyone has never learned to trust anyone.

840. Man gazes upon the stars, desiring to reach them. There is one star, though often neglected, he can reach (Revelation 22:16).[173]

841. God is watching you.

842. A life full of empty moments cannot be called life.

843. A man tagged out at the plate cannot bring home the winning run no matter how close he came to scoring.

844. A master chef has no need for recipes.

845. Men look up to and admire the accomplished professional, but have no clue of what they themselves could one day be.

846. Tragedies in life are standing in line to take place because the Devil has separately planned each and every one of them (John 10:10).[174]

847. Are all the convicted guilty?

848. Though long and painful the night, joy cometh in the "mourning."

849. The building is sanctified if the people in it are.

850. Jesus ... take a drink. Refreshing, isn't he?

851. Leaders are decision makers. Decision makers are leaders.

852. The ears hear, the eyes see, the tongue speaks.

853. Involving oneself in the labor of procrastination is much more difficult and time consuming than just going ahead and doing what has to be done.

854. Money is a covering for the wicked.

855. In their interactions with one another, toddlers make more sense than grown adults do.

856. God is not important until his name is being screamed out to for help.

857. Stolen items are invisible gain.

858. Champions many times emerge, at best, only by inches over their opponents.[175]

859. Claim it.

860. Let the huddled masses raise up their standard in protest to rich rule.

861. Believe what you imagine.

862. There is a God.

863. Unlike the Supreme Court, with the Holy Trinity every decision is unanimous!

864. The physical heart works ceaselessly to keep the body alive but is never given praise; nor is it given thanks for doing so.

865. Morning glories lift up their arms in worship to God at the same time each day.

866. Beware of those who boast.

867. Each time you make it to the end of another day, God saved your life.

868. Each child is a new nation.

869. In a hurry to get there? Pause ... take a breath.

870. Being burned alive is an excruciating and painful way to die. Hell (fire) is the most excruciating and painful way to die forever.

871. The Word of God transforms lives and turns destinies.

872. Christ's suffering was a free gift, but not for him.

873. Some of us are too educated to learn.

874. After journeying abroad I one day returned, less the man I was, but more the man I had come to be.

875. Every time one looks up from within himself growth takes place.

876. Fairness redistributes the playing field.

877. The intellect is as a tinkling cymbal when not balanced with love (1 Corinthians 13:1).[176]

878. There's no more a fruitful sacrifice of a parent to a child than their presence, in any measure, of quality time.

At all hours they watch over you. They are your …
Guardian Angels
(Local Police Departments)

Guardian angels are watching your way;
Guardian angels by night and by day.
Guardian angels whose weapons are drawn.
Courage and valor, to its force they belong.
Guardians stand by, are ready to fall
To give you their futures, their lives, and their all.
Guardians choosing not who to protect,
Against evil's bidding they stand tall, erect.
Guardian watchmen their numbers are few,
Will surrender their lives at any moment for you.
Today they are spat on and despised; they are cursed.
But in Satan's destruction, their arrival is first!
Guardians, who in the world have sent you?

A God who is loving, a God who is true;
A God who protects, a God who defends,
A God who is with us though other things end.
A God who sends angels, guarding your way,
Guardian angels by night and by day.
Guardian angels whose weapons are drawn.
Purple hearts born of courage
who have come and have gone.
Remember, oh people, whatever you do,
That guardian angels on this earth protect you,
And petition by prayer the Lord God above
Will carry them safely each day by his love.
Those guardian angels who stand daily by,
Between you and danger and never ask why.

879. To find success, dig deep into your heart.

880. You cannot force-feed another's growth.

881. Faith sees into the future.

882. Flattery is the oil that fills the lamp of foolish pride.

883. The guiltless are (Matthew 12:7).[177]

884. The wicked man's prosperity erects a city that will never be realized.

885. A bright idea is not always a good idea.

886. As personalities clash, nitro meets glycerin!

887. Free … dumb; free … dumb.

888. A timely word must be received in a timely fashion.

889. No matter how little the light, there is no amount of darkness that can blot it out.

A continuous vigil will the …
Steeple Keep

Steeple, steeple, steeple, keep thy pinnacle on high,
Establish it to stand erect before each watching eye.
Steeple ever point the way, teach men that there can be
But one direction and one hope
to loose the bands and set men free.
Steeple solemn ere you stand
with but one thought in mind,
With single hope that men on earth
one day their God will find.
So stand tall steeple, steeple keep
thy pinnacle on high.
Thy commission is to point the way.
"Come to God," thy silent cry.

890. That which is yours needn't be taken by force.

891. Prayer supercharges one's vessel.

892. A replacement idea for two people separating for a while to think about things is … ending the relationship.

893. Simple math: death is not always the subtraction of life.

894. You won't see it coming!

895. Have you prayed today?

896. Prayer is but a thought from man sent in God's direction.

897. No matter how many flawed men live, God's intent and purpose will be still be established!

898. To that which is eternal always is.

899. Big people are really little people with big ideas.

900. Greed has no cure.

Contrary to popular belief …
Money Doesn't Make You Rich

Money doesn't make you rich; it only serves to be
A tool when kept well in its place,
Otherwise a form of slavery.
For some people think importance
Is weighed in dollar bills,
But having millions in the bank
Leaves your soul impoverished still.
Money can't buy happiness.
Though you get all you can get,
You still lack peace and wonder why,
For of simple things you are in debt.
So … money doesn't make you rich;
It's just the things you do.
With wealth or not, sow good in life,
And you'll be rich your whole life through.

901. Damage control? You waited too long.

902. Hidden away inside of every individual is one's true nature.

903. Every seed is a sleeper cell.

904. The one constant in writing is rewriting.

905. The seas yield an abundant harvest. So, too, does truth and righteousness.

906. Some of the best of us were once some of the worst of us.

907. Doubt paves the way to an uncertain future.

908. You still have time.

909. Joy in the soul makes the eyes smile.

910. The man who loves lives by what he loves.

911. As vast as the oceans of the world are being populated by myriad creatures (many yet undiscovered), they are only part of what God holds in his hand!

912. A vocally talented attorney can talk the wool off a sheep and then pull it over the eyes of a jury.

913. At the end of a workday a man gets to go home. At the end of his career, he gets to retire. At the end of his life, he gets to do both.

914. The more money there is to be made, the more hands there are in the pot.

915. Through man's imagination he is afforded large living spaces.

916. The United States is a divided humanity.

917. Everest is a gamble … Why gamble?

918. Bypass truth, and you will suffer the consequences.

919. Near-death experiences? Life without Christ is always that.

920. A red traffic signal means stop. So does a string of very bad luck.

921. Jealousy believes its every suspicion.

922. Writing is not simply a process of copying words onto a piece of paper. Writing is a chrysalis in which is contained a collection of words, each having their own singular meaning. When mingled together, they undergo a process of translation, or metamorphosis, bringing about a total change in their collective meaning. This process, or fusion, begets a new creation, a creation birthed by the writer's passionate desire to bring into existence something new and distinct, something never before seen on earth.

923. The power of thought is literally capable of bringing into existence not yet realized material substance (Hebrews 11:1).[178]

924. If you don't believe in what you can't see, why make plans for tomorrow?

925. Desire is the origin of beginnings.

They are a relentless army as …
They March, They Come

They march, they come … two … three … four …
"To the left! … To the left! … To the left! …
To the left!"
Their invasion is without mercy and without respect of persons.
Intruding, they advance into our homes …
"Compane-e-e-e … halt!"
They march … they come … they come.

926. Satan was never once human.

927. At one point in my life I was not like *The Little Train that Could*. I was more like the little train that thought he couldn't.

928. What color is a man?

929. Why look for something your heart is not looking for?

Including unimportant things in one's life and leaving
out those things that are important is …
An Extravagant Waste

Life is an extravagant waste when you are
concerned about things and not people.
Life is an extravagant waste when you worry about the things
you don't have instead of appreciating the things you do.
Life is an extravagant waste when you dream of
greatness but aren't willing to work to attain it.
Life is an extravagant waste when you have a
wife, but your eye is on somebody else's.
Life is an extravagant waste when you complain, complain, complain.

Life is an extravagant waste when your friends' concerns
take priority over those of your children.
Life is an extravagant waste when you wake up each
morning not thinking you are blessed.
Life is an extravagant waste when you don't feel your neighbor's pain.
Life is an extravagant waste when you work hard for what you
earn but willingly gamble it away for nothing in return.
Life is an extravagant waste, an extravagant waste, an extravagant waste.
Life is an extravagant waste.

930. There are certain things that a man in love does. There are certain things that a man not in love doesn't do.

931. When somebody attacks you verbally, and they don't have a reason … they have a reason.

932. Smart is not how much intelligence you have; smart is how much intelligence you use.

933. When the hands are idle, the Devil's workshop is not.

934. Christmas Day is not the only time we should give to others.

935. A person who takes their own life takes only their opportunity for eternal life.

936. Taste and preferences define the individual.

937. God deals with man on a case by case basis.

938. A man sails on the wings of his dreams.

939. Of basketball: all it is a metal ring, and all they're trying to do is put a ball through it. It is not life. It is not salvation. For all ball games … ditto.

940. When perisheth the life in this plane, life springs forth in the next anew.

941. When a man is bound in fetters of iron, there is hope for him of one day escaping them. But for the man enslaved to his own desires,

there is no such hope, for the prison depriving him liberty is of his own design and his love for the trappings of that prison deny him any possibility of escape.

The Empty Cup

The man, while he sipped his morning coffee, read a few short lines from that morning's newspaper about the tragic and untimely deaths of several persons who were residents in his city. The article briefly described how tragically they had perished the night before. Now, the following morning, the same man was quite unavailable for his morning coffee, having met with a fate similar to those he read about the morning before. No doubt, there were a number of persons who, while they sipped their morning coffee, read articles from the same newspaper, which might surely have described in a few short words the tragic and untimely death of our friend from the morning before.

942. A man's stature does not necessarily reflect the size of his ideas.

943. Stop!

944. Your salvation is already paid for.

945. God is the first cause. Man is the second.

946. In God's creation of man, God sculpted magnificence and beauty. In man's (mis)handling of God's beauty and magnificence, he brought upon himself misery and death.

947. Books talk. Experience teaches.

948. What a man's heart holds is what his life unfolds.

949. Responsible people follow rules and regulations.

950. Stories are created to be written in books. Books are written to carry to every man, the story. Of the story, it is expected for man to absorb

its idea and utilize it as a ritual part of his own experience. Finally, it is man's duty to pass the substance of a great story on to other men who, hopefully, will do the same.

951.   Our religion is alive only when we practice all of its beliefs.

952.   Binary code is a system of numbers, commands, and letters that use only two representations, 1 and 0. The entire computer communications system is based entirely on the unseen 1s and 0s. "Now a mediator is not a mediator of one, but God is one" (Galatians 3:20). Ones add up to what is a countless amount. Zeros add up to nothing.

The life of the man who loses everything adds up to zero and, therefore, adds up to nothing. "For what shall it profit a man, if he shall gain the whole world, and lose his own soul (Mark 8:36)?" God's communication to us (his law) "adds up." Ignorance of his communications to us by his law adds up to nothing.

A Future Framed

Your future's framed, repeat, repeat.
A hushed repose to ever keep.
Thy sun is cloud, thy pleasure ... pain,
A joyless soul's oft sad refrain.
Your fate is sealed; there's no return.
Of death's abode you'll ever learn ...
Not sleep, nor rest, but pale unknown,
Whose veil-like shadows are ever shown.
The dread of night forever looms,
By Lucifer, thy soul's entombed;
And no escape's afforded thee,
To be tis sweet ... but not for thee!
In shadow ... cold, you will remain,
Unconscious? ... no! ... forever sane.

What's seen's so real, so here and now,
While tortured millions, as one, avow …
"Why'd we believe that which was vain?
Why'd we accept what was not gain?
We now in morbid sin and guilt
Destroy the house that Christ had built."
A future framed, O' silent sleep,
A hushed repose we'll ever keep.
Our souls be as a tacit tale,
Forever's endless seas to sail.
Life's tomorrow will never be.
It lies deaf to every sinner's plea.
Tomorrow's chapter? There's nothing left
But empty sorrow and thy soul bereft.
Your future's framed; you'd be well to know,
The vast abyss into which you go,
That is the endless night of hell below.

The First Two Steps
of a Thousand-Mile Journey

If I begin, no end in sight
To peer within the black of night.
What I desire but cannot see
That things exist that cannot be.
But I determined soul toward
To thee begotten Son, O Lord;
So written in thy promised Word
That things are seen once they are heard.
The first two steps of many thousands are
Against life's horizon, viewed from afar.
By faith, left is doubt that is then no more seen,
My desire ever present as I will what I dream!

Step, step multiplied many times as desired,
I gained but the things to which I aspired.
Step after step, if only inches are gained,
Means less of my journey before me remains.
One step and two … now my journey's begun,
A determined completion of the race I must run.
With God in my sight, my life's vision is clear;
That my thousand-mile journey's finish is near!
Step, step … two, three, four …

The building process would be lost …

If Dreams Were Made

If dreams were made where dreams come true,
Then there'd be no dreams for me or for you.
For if dreams were made where their end be found,
What goal would we have for hope to surround?
If we had not invisible things to reach for,
With heaven not seen, who'd walk through its door?
Without faith and its vision to lock in on dreams,
No man on earth could reach the supreme.
Make what's imagined, and imagine it so.
How can this be done? Be still, and you'll know.
But temper direction with the wisdom of God,
And you'll never tire from toil on any path that you trod.
So simple defies it the logic of man,
As a child can believe it; if you believe it, you can!
Many mountains un-scaled, and no new worlds unfold,
The riches you lose are Earth's bounty untold!
My child, lend an ear, and by your heart you'll perceive,
That your dreams will come true if you simply believe!
And if dreams were made where dreams come true,
With everything done, there'd be nothing to do.

For if the goal would appear at the instant you dream,
Determination, faith, and patience
would be all lost it seems.
So that dreams are not made where their end doth be found,
This is God's great design, and I might add, profound!

I see you in the mirror …
All the World's Faces Are Mine

The face of the Asian is my face;
The face of the European, too.
The face of any nation, whatever custom or tone,
The face that I see in the mirror is you.
Whether Africa or China, Greenland, or Spain,
Italy, South America, or France,
We should all get along (Rodney King),
try to help the world's souls,
Instead of killing each other by war's strange romance.
The face of the Eskimo, though formed different than mine,
Embraces a soul just like me.
Though foreign the faces of the world that surrounds,
When I look in those faces, it's myself that I see.

My teacher and example was suddenly …
Plucked Away to Beauty

God plucked his flower while still in bloom,
Afore it wilt away;
While young and strong with petals bright,
To a higher dawn, t'ward his blessed light.
God taken 'way the rose of him
That was so proudly set

123

Inside the garden of our hearts,
The man of God we'd met.
Erased 'twas earth, transformed he at
The twinkling of an eye;
Our prophet Mack, God lifted him
In fire toward the sky!
So dry your eyes, my daughters,
And weep me not my heart.
He lived his life before us,
His laughing smile will ne'er depart.
This man, the work of God did he,
Rejoice, for Rev. Mack is free[179]!

I wish it would come to an end, but I know I'll be …

Waiting Forever

Waiting forever, but a change will not come.
Begging forgiveness of God's only Son.
Seeking death's shoreline from its sea vast and wide,
Finding it never though forever I've tried.
With no rest before me and forever no peace,
The torments I suffer I know shall not cease.
Had I given my life to the Savior of all.
I'd have peace forever had I heeded his call.
"Come to me ye that labor, and ye shall find rest,
Surrender your souls, oh my children, be blessed!"
But, too late came my answer, and the point is now moot.
My salvation's behind me as my life bore no fruit.
Now I'm waiting forever, but a change will not come,
And I'm begging forgiveness of God's only Son.
I know he would pardon if only he could.
The things he commanded were well understood.
I've discovered no rest from death's sea, vast and wide,

Since I'd chosen the other alternative … pride.
I'll suffer forever the torments of hell,
Knowing there'll never be a finishing bell.
No rest there forever, bound by death's endless chain,
In the black of hell's night, I shall forever remain.

Only …
If

If we had no way of knowing
how the sun shows forth its beauty,
If we had no way of knowing
how the rivers run so truly,
If we had no time or reason
to get out of bed each day,
There would still be life that's given us
Always a path to light our way.
If the Rocky Mountain ranges
did not ascend to God in song,
If living creatures with desire
for life's tomorrow did not long,
If the bees did not make honey,
nor the world its love portrayed …
We would still quite daily marvel
at all the things that God has made.
If the earth did never yield to us
its fruit abundantly,
If the mist of morning dew
forbid its diamond drops to see,
And each flower hid its beauty
in their elegant parade,
My breath would still be taken
at the wonder life displayed.

How the spider looms its palaces,
or a serpent on a rock (Proverbs 30:19).[180]
How the birds, no captain evident,
are a regimented flock,
How the ocean with its mysteries
hath not revealed its soul
To be near the Creator of all this
would be my most chief aim and goal.
If we had no way of knowing,
if these things were not yet clear,
If we had no way to understand
how the manifest appears,
If we just would think how anything
on earth could ever be,
We'd acknowledge how our God
has made all things so wondrously!

Endnotes

1 "Now faith is the substance of things hoped for, the evidence of things not seen" (PhPrv 3; Hebrews 11:1).

2 "For the love of money is the root of all evil: which while some coveted after, they have erred from the faith, and pierced themselves through with many sorrows" (PhPrv 15; 1 Timothy 6:10).

3 "Thou shalt not bow down thyself to them, nor serve them: for I the Lord thy God am a jealous God, visiting the iniquity of the fathers upon the children unto the third and fourth generation of them that hate me;" (PhPrv 26; Exodus 20:5).

4 "And when he was demanded of the Pharisees, when the kingdom of God should come, he answered them and said, The kingdom of God cometh not with observation: Neither shall they say, Lo here! or, lo there! for, behold, the kingdom of God is within you" (PhPrv 27; Luke 17:20, 21).

5 "Howbeit he would not hearken unto her voice: but, being stronger than she, forced her, and lay with her. Then Amnon hated her exceedingly; so that the hatred wherewith he hated her was greater than the love wherewith he had loved her. And Amnon said unto her, Arise, be gone" (PhPrv 32; 2 Samuel 13:14, 15).

6 "Now faith is the substance of things hoped for, the evidence of things not seen" (PhPrv 35; Hebrews 11:1).

7 "And said, Naked came I out of my mother's womb, and naked shall I return thither: the Lord gave, and the Lord hath taken away; blessed be the name of the Lord" (PhPrv 44; Job 1:21).

8 "Before the mountains were brought forth, or ever thou hadst formed the earth and the world, even from everlasting to everlasting, thou art God" (PhPrv 47; Psalm 90:2).

9 "And when he was demanded of the Pharisees, when the kingdom of God should come, he answered them and said, The kingdom of God cometh not with observation: Neither shall they say, Lo here! or, lo there! for, behold, the kingdom of God is within you" (PhPrv 48; Luke 17:20–21).

10. "Take my yoke upon you, and learn of me; for I am meek and lowly in heart: and ye shall find rest unto your souls…" (PhPrv 61; Matthew 11:29).

11. "That they may keep thee from the strange woman, from the stranger which flattereth with her words. For at the window of my house I looked through my casement, And beheld among the simple ones, I discerned among the youths, a young man void of understanding …" (PhPrv 62; Proverbs 7:5–7).

12. "Thou shalt not kill." (PhPrv 65; Exodus 20:13).

13. "And God created great whales, and every living creature that moveth, which the waters brought forth abundantly, after their kind, and every winged fowl after his kind: and God saw that it was good" (PhPrv 66; Genesis 1:21).

14. And the Lord God took the man, and put him into the garden of Eden to dress it and to keep it" (PhPrv 67, Genesis 2:15).

15. "Set your affection on things above, not on things on the earth" (PhPrv 72; Colossians 3:2).

16. "Now faith is the substance of things hoped for, the evidence of things not seen" (Poem "A Dream"; Hebrews 11:1).

17. "Then answered Jesus and said unto them, Verily, verily, I say unto you, The Son can do nothing of himself, but what he seeth the Father do: for what things soever he doeth, these also doeth the Son likewise" (PhPrv 98; John 5:19).

18. "There is no fear in love; but perfect love casteth out fear: because fear hath torment. He that feareth is not made perfect in love" (PhPrv 102; 1 John 4:18).

19. "Now faith is the substance of things hoped for, the evidence of things not seen" (PhPrv 103; Hebrews 11:1. Also look up the definition of "quantum physics).

20. "The heart is deceitful above all things, and desperately wicked: who can know it?" (PhPrv 116; Jeremiah 17:9).

21. "And I say also unto thee, That thou art Peter, and upon this rock I will build my church; and the gates of hell shall not prevail against it" (PhPrv 119; Matthew 16:18).

22. "Now the serpent was more subtil than any beast of the field which the Lord God had made. And he said unto the woman, Yea, hath God said, Ye shall not eat of every tree of the garden?" (PhPrv 120; Genesis 3:1).

23. "Finally, brethren, whatsoever things are true, whatsoever things *are* honest, whatsoever things *are* just, whatsoever things *are* pure, whatsoever things *are* lovely, whatsoever things *are* of good report; if *there be* any virtue, and if *there be* any praise, think on these things" (PhPrv 121; Philippians 4:8).

24. "Be not deceived; God is not mocked: for whatsoever a man soweth, that shall he also reap" (PhPrv 122; Galatians 6:7).

25. "And David said to Saul, Let no man's heart fail because of him; thy servant will go and fight with this Philistine" (PhPrv127; 1 Samuel 17:32).

26   "Then he which had received the one talent came and said, Lord, I knew thee that thou art an hard man, reaping where thou hast not sown, and gathering where thou hast not strawed: And I was afraid, and went and hid thy talent in the earth: lo, there thou hast that is thine. His lord answered and said unto him, Thou wicked and slothful servant, thou knewest that I reap where I sowed not, and gather where I have not strawed: Thou oughtest therefore to have put my money to the exchangers, and then at my coming I should have received mine own with usury. Take therefore the talent from him, and give it unto him which hath ten talents. For unto every one that hath shall be given, and he shall have abundance: but from him that hath not shall be taken away even that which he hath. And cast ye the unprofitable servant into outer darkness: there shall be weeping and gnashing of teeth" (PhPrv 132; Matthew 25:24–30).

27   "Then Pilate therefore took Jesus, and scourged him" (PhPrv 135; John 19:1).

28   "For this cause I Paul, the prisoner of Jesus Christ for you Gentiles …" (PhPrv 136; Ephesians 3:1).

29   "For God speaketh once, yea twice, yet man perceiveth it not. In a dream, in a vision of the night, when deep sleep falleth upon men, in slumberings upon the bed; Then he openeth the ears of men, and sealeth their instruction, …" (PhPrv 137; Job 33:14–16).

30   "He that receiveth you receiveth me, and he that receiveth me receiveth him that sent me. In math: Things equal to the same thing are equal to each other" (the reflexive axiom) (PhPrv 138; Matthew 10:40).

31   "Thou shalt not take the name of the Lord thy God in vain; for the Lord will not hold him guiltless that taketh his name in vain" (PhPrv 139; Exodus 20:7).

32   "Not that which goeth into the mouth defileth a man; but that which cometh out of the mouth, this defileth a man" (PhPrv 142; Matthew 15:11).

33   "Being filled with all unrighteousness, fornication, wickedness, covetousness, maliciousness; full of envy, murder, debate, deceit, malignity; whisperers, …" (PhPrv 144; Romans 1:29)

34   "The wicked borroweth, and payeth not again: but the righteous sheweth mercy, and giveth" (PhPrv 146; Psalms 37:21).

35   "And straightway the father of the child cried out, and said with tears, Lord, I believe; help thou mine unbelief (PhPrv148; Mark 9:24).

36   "For since the beginning of the world men have not heard, nor perceived by the ear, neither hath the eye seen, O God, beside thee, what he hath prepared for him that waiteth for him."

"But as it is written, Eye hath not seen, nor ear heard, neither have entered into the heart of man, the things which God hath prepared for them that love him" (PhPrv 149; Isaiah 64:4; 1 Corinthians 2:9).

37   "So the servants of the householder came and said unto him, Sir, didst not thou sow good seed in thy field? from whence then hath it tares? He said unto them, An enemy hath done this. The servants said unto him, Wilt thou then that we go and gather them up? (PhPrv 152; Matthew 13:27, 28).

38   "And the Lord God formed man of the dust of the ground, and breathed into his nostrils the breath of life; and man became a living soul" (PhPrv 153; Genesis 2:7).

39   "And Jesus answered him, saying, It is written, That man shall not live by bread alone, but by every word of God" (PhPrv 159; Luke 4:4).

40   "Ask, and it shall be given you; seek, and ye shall find; knock, and it shall be opened unto you:" (PhPrv 160; Matthew 7:7).

41   "And God said, Let us make man in our image, after our likeness: and let them have dominion over the fish of the sea, and over the fowl of the air, and over the cattle, and over all the earth, and over every creeping thing that creepeth upon the earth. So God created man in his own image, in the image of God created he him; male and female created he them" (PhPrv 162; Genesis 1:26, 27).

42   "How art thou fallen from heaven, O Lucifer, son of the morning! how art thou cut down to the ground, which didst weaken the nations! For thou hast said in thine heart, I will ascend into heaven, I will exalt my throne above the stars of God: I will sit also upon the mount of the congregation, in the sides of the north: I will ascend above the heights of the clouds; I will be like the most High. Yet thou shalt be brought down to hell, to the sides of the pit" (PhPrv 163; Isaiah 14:12–15)."

43   "Thou hast given him his heart's desire, and hast not withholden the request of his lips. Selah" ("Promise Bend"; Psalm 21:2).

44   "For nation shall rise against nation, and kingdom against kingdom: and there shall be famines, and pestilences, and earthquakes, in divers places" (PhPrv 169; Matthew 24:7).

45   "There is a way which seemeth right unto a man, but the end thereof are the ways of death" (PhPrv 172; Proverbs 14:12).

46   "And he spake a parable unto them, saying, The ground of a certain rich man brought forth plentifully: And he thought within himself, saying, What shall I do, because I have no room where to bestow my fruits? And he said, This will I do: I will pull down my barns, and build greater; and there will I bestow all my fruits and my goods. And I will say to my soul, Soul, thou hast much goods laid up for many years; take thine ease, eat, drink, and be merry. But God said unto him, Thou fool, this night thy soul shall be required of thee: then whose shall those things be, which thou hast provided?" (PhPrv 190; Luke 12:16–20)."

47   "Cease from anger, and forsake wrath: fret not thyself in any wise to do evil" (PhPrv 191; Psalm 37:8).

48   "O generation of vipers, how can ye, being evil, speak good things? for out of the abundance of the heart the mouth speaketh" (PhPrv 194; Matthew 12:34).

49   "And he received them at their hand, and fashioned it with a graving tool, after he had made it a molten calf: and they said, These be thy gods, O Israel, which brought thee up out of the land of Egypt" (PhPrv 198; Exodus 32:4).

50   "The thing that hath been, it is that which shall be; and that which is done is that which shall be done: and there is no new thing under the sun" ("Our Land Is Cursed"; Ecclesiastes 1:9).

51   "I charge thee therefore before God, and the Lord Jesus Christ, who shall judge the quick and the dead at his appearing and his kingdom" ("Our Land Is Cursed"; 2 Timothy 4:1).

52   "Ask, and it shall be given you; seek, and ye shall find; knock, and it shall be opened unto you" ("Our Land Is Cursed"; Matthew 7:7).

53   "In the same hour came forth fingers of a man's hand, and wrote over against the candlestick upon the plaister of the wall of the king's palace: and the king saw the part of the hand that wrote" ("Our Land Is Cursed"; Daniel 5:5).

54   "Pilate saith unto him, What is truth? And when he had said this, he went out again unto the Jews, and saith unto them, I find in him no fault at all."

     "When Pilate saw that he could prevail nothing, but that rather a tumult was made, he took water, and washed his hands before the multitude, saying, I am innocent of the blood of this just person: see ye to it" (PhPrv 203; John 18:38; Matthew 27:24).

55   "What is man, that thou art mindful of him? and the son of man, that thou visitest him?" (PhPrv 208; Psalm 8:4).

56   "Thou preparest a table before me in the presence of mine enemies: thou anointest my head with oil; my cup runneth over" ("Love Is Not Extreme"; Psalm 23:5).

57   "So God created man in his own image, in the image of God created he him; male and female created he them" (PhPrv 217; Genesis 1:27).

58   "And not only so, but we glory in tribulations also: knowing that tribulation worketh patience; And patience, experience; and experience, hope: And hope maketh not ashamed; because the love of God is shed abroad in our hearts by the Holy Ghost which is given unto us" (PhPrv 219; Romans 5:3–5).

59   (… souls sell?) "For ye are bought with a price: therefore glorify God in your body, and in your spirit, which are God's" ("Peace that Is in Pieces"; 1 Corinthians 6:20).

60   "(… and might) Then he answered and spake unto me, saying, This is the word of the Lord unto Zedrubbabel, saying, Not by might, nor by power, but by my spirit, saith the Lord of hosts" (Zechariah 4:6).

61   "(... ignored call) Jesus saith unto him, I am the way, the truth, and the life: no man cometh unto the Father, but by me (John 14:6).

62   "But the other answering rebuked him, saying, Dost not thou fear God, seeing thou art in the same condemnation? And we indeed justly; for we receive the due reward of our deeds: but this man hath done nothing amiss. And he said unto Jesus, Lord, remember me when thou comest into thy kingdom. And Jesus said unto him, Verily I say unto thee, Today shalt thou be with me in paradise" (PhPrv 223; Luke 23:40–43).

63   "For the wages of sin is death; but the gift of God is eternal life through Jesus Christ our Lord" (PhPrv 224; Romans 6:23).

64   "Heaven and earth shall pass away, but my words shall not pass away (PhPrv 225; Matthew 24:35).

65   "But wilt thou know, O vain man, that faith without works is dead? (PhPrv 242; James 2:20).

66   "Charity suffereth long, and is kind; charity envieth not; charity vaunteth not itself, is not puffed up" (PhPrv 250; 1 Corinthians 13:4).

67   "Whereas ye know not what shall be on the morrow. For what is your life? It is even a vapour, that appeareth for a little time, and then vanisheth away" ("Gone a Far Journey"; James 4:14).

68   "Not every one that saith unto me, Lord, Lord, shall enter into the kingdom of heaven; but he that doeth the will of my Father which is in heaven" (PhPrv 252; Matthew 7:21).

69   "Beloved, think it not strange concerning the fiery trial which is to try you, as though some strange thing happened unto you: But rejoice, inasmuch as ye are partakers of Christ's sufferings; that, when his glory shall be revealed, ye may be glad also with exceeding joy" ("Even in the Darkness"; 1 Peter 4:12–13).

70   "For nothing is secret, that shall not be made manifest; neither any thing hid, that shall not be known and come abroad" (PhPrv 256; Luke 8:17).

71   "And fear not them which kill the body, but are not able to kill the soul: but rather fear him which is able to destroy both soul and body in hell" (PhPrv 258; Matthew 10:28).

72   "Be still, and know that I am God: I will be exalted among the heathen, I will be exalted in the earth" ("It Starts with a Dream"; Psalm 46:10).

73   "With her much fair speech she caused him to yield, with the flattering of her lips she forced him" (PhPrv 261; Proverbs 7:21).

74   "For verily I say unto you, That whosoever shall say unto this mountain, Be thou removed, and be thou cast into the sea; and shall not doubt in his heart, but shall believe that those things which he saith shall come to pass; he shall have whatsoever he saith. Therefore I say unto you, 'What things soever ye desire,

when ye pray, believe that ye receive them, and ye shall have them'" (PhPrv 262; Mark 11:23–24).

75   "The Lord is my shepherd; I shall not want" (PhPrv 265; Psalm 23:1).

76   "Even so the tongue is a little member, and boasteth great things. Behold, how great a matter a little fire kindleth! And the tongue is a fire, a world of iniquity: so is the tongue among our members, that it defileth the whole body, and setteth on fire the course of nature; and it is set on fire of hell" (PhPrv 269; James 3:5–6).

77   "And there was war in heaven: Michael and his angels fought against the dragon; and the dragon fought and his angels" (PhPrv 286; Revelation 12:7).

78   "Whereas ye know not what shall be on the morrow. For what is your life? It is even a vapour, that appeareth for a little time, and then vanisheth away" ("David Died"; James 4:14).

79   "Now faith is the substance of things hoped for, the evidence of things not seen. (PhPrv 296; Hebrews 11:1).

80   "For God so loved the world, that he gave his only begotten Son, that whosoever believeth in him should not perish, but have everlasting life" ("A Little Town Called Bethlehem"; John 3:16).

81   "For the wages of sin is death; but the gift of God is eternal life through Jesus Christ our Lord" (PhPrv 318; Romans 6:23).

82   "Every good gift and every perfect gift is from above, and cometh down from the Father of lights, with whom is no variableness, neither shadow of turning" (PhPrv 323; James 1:17).

83   "Whosoever therefore shall break one of these least commandments, and shall teach men so, he shall be called the least in the kingdom of heaven: but whosoever shall do and teach them, the same shall be called great in the kingdom of heaven" (PhPrv 329; Matthew 5:19).

84   "And when the woman saw that the tree [was] good for food, and that it [was] pleasant to the eyes, and a tree to be desired to make [one] wise, she took of the fruit thereof, and did eat, and gave also unto her husband with her; and he did eat. And the eyes of them both were opened, and they knew that they [were] naked; and they sewed fig leaves together, and made themselves aprons" (PhPrv 330; Genesis 3:6, 7).

85   "And they say unto him, We have here but five loaves, and two fishes. He said, Bring them hither to me. And he commanded the multitude to sit down on the grass, and took the five loaves, and the two fishes, and looking up to heaven, he blessed, and brake, and gave the loaves to his disciples, and the disciples to the multitude. And they did all eat, and were filled: and they took up of the fragments that remained twelve baskets full. And they that had eaten were

about five thousand men, beside women and children" (PhPrv 335; Matthew 14:17–21).

86 "Ye have heard that it was said by them of old time, Thou shalt not commit adultery: But I say unto you, That whosoever looketh on a woman to lust after her hath committed adultery with her already in his heart" (PhPrv 336; Matthew 5:27, 28).

87 "How art thou fallen from heaven, O Lucifer, son of the morning! how art thou cut down to the ground, which didst weaken the nations! For thou hast said in thine heart, I will ascend into heaven, I will exalt my throne above the stars of God: I will sit also upon the mount of the congregation, in the sides of the north: I will ascend above the heights of the clouds; I will be like the most High. Yet thou shalt be brought down to hell, to the sides of the pit" ("Fallen"; Isaiah 14:12–15).

88 "And he saith unto them, Follow me, and I will make you fishers of men" (PhPrv 353; Matthew 4:19).

89 "Against thee, thee only, have I sinned, and done *this* evil in thy sight: that thou mightest be justified when thou speakest, *and* be clear when thou judgest" (PhPrv 355; Psalm 51:4).

90 "That ye may be the children of your Father which is in heaven: for he maketh his sun to rise on the evil and on the good, and sendeth rain on the just and on the unjust" (PhPrv 358; Matthew 5:45).

91 "For whosoever will save his life shall lose it: and whosoever will lose his life for my sake shall find it" (PhPrv 360; Matthew 16:25).

92 "Now faith is the substance of things hoped for, the evidence of things not seen" (PhPrv 372; Hebrews 11:1).

93 "And these are they likewise which are sown on stony ground; who, when they have heard the word, immediately receive it with gladness; And have no root in themselves, and so endure but for a time: afterward, when affliction or persecution ariseth for the word's sake, immediately they are offended" ("A Modern Bore"; Mark 4:16, 17).

94 "Now faith is the substance of things hoped for, the evidence of things not seen" ("That's What Faith Will Do for You"; Hebrews 11:1).

95 "And such were some of you: but ye are washed, but ye are sanctified, but ye are justified in the name of the Lord Jesus, and by the Spirit of our God" (PhPrv 392; 1 Corinthians 6:11).

96 "For this corruptible must put on incorruption, and this mortal must put on immortality" ("Gravestones Strewn"; 1 Corinthians 15:53).

97 "And if ye salute your brethren only, what do ye more than others? do not even the publicans so?" (PhPrv 412; Matthew 5:47).

98   "For the Lamb which is in the midst of the throne shall feed them, and shall lead them unto living fountains of waters: and God shall wipe away all tears from their eyes" ("Loved Ones Passed"; Revelation 7:17).

99   "But he that shall blaspheme against the Holy Ghost hath never forgiveness, but is in danger of eternal damnation" (PhPrv 420; Mark 3:29).

100   "Again, ye have heard that it hath been said by them of old time, Thou shalt not forswear thyself, but shalt perform unto the Lord thine oaths: But I say unto you, Swear not at all; neither by heaven; for it is God's throne: Nor by the earth; for it is his footstool: neither by Jerusalem; for it is the city of the great King. Neither shalt thou swear by thy head, because thou canst not make one hair white or black. But let your communication be, Yea, yea; Nay, nay: for whatsoever is more than these cometh of evil" (PhPrv 421; Matthew 5:33–37).

101   "Verily, verily, I say unto you, He that entereth not by the door into the sheepfold, but climbeth up some other way, the same is a thief and a robber" ("The Happy Doorway"; John 10:1).

102   "And the whole multitude sought to touch him: for there went virtue out of him, and healed them all" (PhPrv 422; Luke 6:19).

103   "Therefore hell hath enlarged herself, and opened her mouth without measure: and their glory, and their multitude, and their pomp, and he that rejoiceth, shall descend into it" (PhPrv 423; Isaiah 5:14).

104   "And when he was demanded of the Pharisees, when the kingdom of God should come, he answered them and said, The kingdom of God cometh not with observation: Neither shall they say, Lo here! or, lo there! for, behold, the kingdom of God is within you. And he said unto the disciples, The days will come, when ye shall desire to see one of the days of the Son of man, and ye shall not see it" (PhPrv 424; Luke 17:20–22).

105   "Teaching them to observe all things whatsoever I have commanded you: and, lo, I am with you always, even unto the end of the world. Amen" (PhPrv 429; Matthew 28:20).

106   "And when he was demanded of the Pharisees, when the kingdom of God should come, he answered them and said, The kingdom of God cometh not with observation: Neither shall they say, Lo here! or, lo there! for, behold, the kingdom of God is within you" (PhPrv 430; Luke 17:20–21).

107   "Except the Lord build the house, they labour in vain that build it: except the Lord keep the city, the watchman waketh but in vain" (PhPrv 434; Psalm 127:1).

108   "And all this assembly shall know that the Lord saveth not with sword and spear: for the battle is the Lord's, and he will give you into our hands" (PhPrv 442; 1 Samuel 17:47).

109   "And Moses answered and said, But, behold, they will not believe me, nor hearken unto my voice: for they will say, The Lord hath not appeared unto thee.

And the Lord said unto him, What [is] that in thine hand? And he said, A rod. And he said, Cast it on the ground. And he cast it on the ground, and it became a serpent; and Moses fled from before it. And the Lord said unto Moses, Put forth thine hand, and take it by the tail. And he put forth his hand, and caught it, and it became a rod in his hand" (PhPrv 445; Exodus 4:1–4).

110 "I Jesus have sent mine angel to testify unto you these things in the churches. I am the root and the offspring of David, and the bright and morning star" (PhPrv 453; Revelation 22:16).

111 "Trust in the Lord with all thine heart; and lean not unto thine own understanding. In all thy ways acknowledge him, and he shall direct thy paths" (PhPrv 463; Proverbs 3:5, 6).

112 "I Jesus have sent mine angel to testify unto you these things in the churches. I am the root and the offspring of David, and the bright and morning star" ("Rising in the East"; Revelation 22:16).

113 "Jesus saith unto him, I am the way, the truth, and the life: no man cometh unto the Father, but by me" (John 14:6).

114 "To him that smote Egypt in their firstborn: for his mercy endureth for ever: And brought out Israel from among them: for his mercy endureth for ever: With a strong hand, and with a stretched out arm: for his mercy endureth for ever. To him which divided the Red sea into parts: for his mercy endureth for ever: And made Israel to pass through the midst of it: for his mercy endureth for ever: But overthrew Pharaoh and his host in the Red sea: for his mercy endureth for ever" (Psalm 136:10–15).

115 "And if it seem evil unto you to serve the Lord, choose you this day whom ye will serve; whether the gods which your fathers served that were on the other side of the flood, or the gods of the Amorites, in whose land ye dwell: but as for me and my house, we will serve the Lord" (Joshua 24:15).

116 "The heart is deceitful above all things, and desperately wicked: who can know it?" (PhPrv 481; Jeremiah 17:9).

117 "Is there no balm in Gilead; is there no physician there? why then is not the health of the daughter of my people recovered?" ("In His Envelope"; Jeremiah 8:22).

118 "And ye shall be hated of all men for my name's sake: but he that endureth to the end shall be saved" (PhPrv 491; Matthew 10:22).

119 "In the midst of the street of it, and on either side of the river, was there the tree of life, which bare twelve manner of fruits, and yielded her fruit every month: and the leaves of the tree were for the healing of the nations" ("Children in Your Garden"; Revelation 22:2).

120 "Thou shalt beat him with the rod, and shalt deliver his soul from hell" (PhPrv 517; Proverbs 23:14).

121 "And Saul said to David, Thou art not able to go against this Philistine to fight with him: for thou art but a youth, and he a man of war from his youth … And the Philistine came on and drew near unto David; and the man that bare the shield went before him. And when the Philistine looked about, and saw David, he disdained him: for he was but a youth, and ruddy, and of a fair countenance" (PhPrv 521; 1 Samuel 17:33, 41–42).

122 "So God created man in his own image, in the image of God created he him; male and female created he them" (PhPrv 530; Genesis 1:27).

123 "There is that maketh himself rich, yet hath nothing: there is that maketh himself poor, yet hath great riches" (PhPrv 533; Proverbs 13:7).

124 "Labour not for the meat which perisheth, but for that meat which endureth unto everlasting life, which the Son of man shall give unto you: for him hath God the Father sealed."

"And it was commanded them that they should not hurt the grass of the earth, neither any green thing, neither any tree; but only those men which have not the seal of God in their foreheads" ("Signed Concealed"; John 6:27; Revelation 9:4).

125 "Let us therefore fear, lest, a promise being left us of entering into his rest, any of you should seem to come short of it" (PhPrv 544; Hebrews 4:1).

126 "Be not deceived; God is not mocked: for whatsoever a man soweth, that shall he also reap" (PhPrv 551; Galatians 6:7).

127 "Jesus saith unto him, I am the way, the truth, and the life: no man cometh unto the Father, but by me" ("Signed Santa Claus"; John 14:6).

128 "And when he saw a fig tree in the way, he came to it, and found nothing thereon, but leaves only, and said unto it, Let no fruit grow on thee henceforward for ever. And presently the fig tree withered away" (PhPrv 553; Matthew 21:19).

129 "And I saw in the right hand of him that sat on the throne a book written within and on the backside, sealed with seven seals."

"And the vision of all is become unto you as the words of a book that is sealed, which men deliver to one that is learned, saying, Read this, I pray thee: and he saith, I cannot; for it is sealed" (Revelation 5:1; Isaiah 29:11).

130 "And when the children of Israel saw it, they said one to another, It is manna: for they wist not what it was. And Moses said unto them, This is the bread which the Lord hath given you to eat" (Exodus 16:15).

131 "Now the serpent was more subtil than any beast of the field which the Lord God had made. And he said unto the woman, Yea, hath God said, Ye shall not eat of every tree of the garden? And the woman said unto the serpent, We may eat of the fruit of the trees of the garden: But of the fruit of the tree which is in the midst of the garden, God hath said, Ye shall not eat of it, neither shall ye touch it, lest ye die. And the serpent said unto the woman, Ye shall not surely

die: For God doth know that in the day ye eat thereof, then your eyes shall be opened, and ye shall be as gods, knowing good and evil. And when the woman saw that the tree was good for food, and that it was pleasant to the eyes, and a tree to be desired to make one wise, she took of the fruit thereof, and did eat, and gave also unto her husband with her; and he did eat" (PhPrv 566; Genesis 3:1–6).

132 "Now no chastening for the present seemeth to be joyous, but grievous: nevertheless afterward it yieldeth the peaceable fruit of righteousness unto them which are exercised thereby" (PhPrv 578; Hebrews 12:11).

133 "For the kingdom of heaven is as a man travelling into a far country, who called his own servants, and delivered unto them his goods. And unto one he gave five talents, to another two, and to another one; to every man according to his several ability; and straightway took his journey" (PhPrv 593; Matthew 25:14–15).

134 "Having a form of godliness, but denying the power thereof: from such turn away" ("They Would Be Ashamed"; 2 Timothy 3:5).

135 "And if thy hand offend thee, cut it off: it is better for thee to enter into live maimed, than having two hands to go into hell, into the fire that never shall be quenched" (Mark 9:43).

136 "For a dream cometh through the multitude of business; and a fool's voice is known by multitude of words" (PhPrv 604; Ecclesiastes 5:3).

137 "Lest I be full, and deny thee, and say, Who is the Lord? or lest I be poor, and steal, and take the name of my God in vain" (PhPrv 605; Proverbs 30:9).

138 "Withhold not correction from the child: for if thou beatest him with the rod, he shall not die. Thou shalt beat him with the rod, and shalt deliver his soul from hell" (PhPrv 610; Proverbs 23:13–14).

139 "For as he thinketh in his heart, so is he: Eat and drink, saith he to thee; but his heart is not with thee" (PhPrv 617; Proverbs 23:7).

140 "And no marvel; for Satan himself is transformed into an angel of light" ("Sin"; 2 Corinthians 11:14).

141 "Watch and pray, that ye enter not into temptation: the spirit indeed is willing, but the flesh is weak" (Matthew 26:41).

142 "There is no fear in love; but perfect love casteth out fear: because fear hath torment. He that feareth is not made perfect in love" (PhPrv 619; 1 John 4:18).

143 "For in many things we offend all. If any man offends not in word, the same is a perfect man, and able also to bridle the whole body" (PhPrv 640; James 3:2).

144 "On the Move. Philadelphia Move Bombing " http://www.phillymag.com/news/2012/05/15/http://www.npr.org/templates/story/story.php?storyId=4651126

145 "To him the porter openeth; and the sheep hear his voice: and he calleth his own sheep by name, and leadeth them out. And when he putteth forth his own

sheep, he goeth before them, and the sheep follow him: for they know his voice. And a stranger will they not follow, but will flee from him: for they know not the voice of strangers" (PhPrv 664; John 10:3–5).

146 "There is no fear in love; but perfect love casteth out fear: because fear hath torment. He that feareth is not made perfect in love" (PhPrv 665; 1 John 4:18).

147 "I saw a dream which made me afraid, and the thoughts upon my bed and the visions of my head troubled me" (PhPrv 666; Daniel 4:5).

148 "Judge not, that ye be not judged" (PhPrv 669; Matthew 7:1).

149 "Behold, all souls are mine; as the soul of the father, so also the soul of the son is mine: the soul that sinneth, it shall die" ("The Corner Gathers"; Ezekiel 18:4).

150 "Thou shalt not covet thy neighbour's house, thou shalt not covet thy neighbour's wife, nor his manservant, nor his maidservant, nor his ox, nor his ass, nor any thing that is thy neighbour's" (PhPrv 678; Exodus 20:17).

151 "For God so loved the world, that he gave his only begotten Son, that whosoever believeth in him should not perish, but have everlasting life" (PhPrv 681; John 3:16).

152 "But God said unto him, Thou fool, this night thy soul shall be required of thee: then whose shall those things be, which thou hast provided?" (PhPrv 683; Luke 12:20).

153 "Cease from anger, and forsake wrath: fret not thyself in any wise to do evil" (PhPrv 692; Psalms 37:8).

154 "Who can find a virtuous woman? for her price is far above rubies" (PhPrv 695; Proverbs 31:10).

155 "I will meditate in thy precepts, and have respect unto thy ways" (PhPrv 703; Psalm 119:15).

156 "Behold, I stand at the door, and knock: if any man hears my voice, and open the door, I will come in to him, and will sup with him, and he with me" (PhPrv 709; Revelation 3:20).

157 "And his raiment became shining, exceeding white as snow; so as no fuller on earth can white them" ("Beloved"; Mark 9:3).

158 "Is there no balm in Gilead; is there no physician there? why then is not the health of the daughter of my people recovered?" (PhPrv 721; Jeremiah 8:22).

159 "Be not deceived; God is not mocked: for whatsoever a man soweth, that shall he also reap" (PhPrv 728; Galatians 6:7).

160 "Thou shalt beat him with the rod, and shalt deliver his soul from hell" (PhPrv 743; Proverbs 23:14).

161 "When the righteous are in authority, the people rejoice: but when the wicked beareth rule, the people mourn" (PhPrv 761; Proverbs 29:2).

162 "And the beast was taken, and with him the false prophet that wrought miracles before him, with which he deceived them that had received the mark of the

beast, and them that worshipped his image. These both were cast alive into a lake of fire burning with brimstone" (PhPrv 771; Revelation 19:20).

163 "The world cannot hate you; but me it hateth, because I testify of it, that the works thereof are evil" (PhPrv 776; John 7:7).

164 "But when he saw the wind boisterous, he was afraid; and beginning to sink, he cried, saying, Lord, save me. And immediately Jesus stretched forth *his* hand, and caught him, and said unto him, O thou of little faith, wherefore didst thou doubt?" (PhPrv 777; Matthew 14:30–31).

165 "Lay not up for yourselves treasures upon earth, where moth and rust doth corrupt, and where thieves break through and steal: But lay up for yourselves treasures in heaven, where neither moth nor rust doth corrupt, and where thieves do not break through nor steal: For where your treasure is, there will your heart be also" (PhPrv 799; Matthew 6:19–21).

166 "For what is a man profited, if he shall gain the whole world, and lose his own soul? or what shall a man give in exchange for his soul?" (PhPrv 804; Matthew 16:26).

167 "I have said, Ye are gods; and all of you are children of the most High" (PhPrv 805; Psalm 82:6).

168 "And they sought to lay hold on him, but feared the people: for they knew that he had spoken the parable against them: and they left him, and went their way." (PhPrv 820; Mark 12:12)

169 "Neither shall they say, Lo here! or, lo there! for, behold, the kingdom of God is within you" (PhPrv 822; Luke 17:21).

170 "And it came to pass at the time of the offering of the evening sacrifice, that Elijah the prophet came near, and said, Lord God of Abraham, Isaac, and of Israel, let it be known this day that thou art God in Israel, and that I am thy servant, and that I have done all these things at thy word. Hear me, O Lord, hear me, that this people may know that thou art the Lord God, and that thou hast turned their heart back again. Then the fire of the Lord fell, and consumed the burnt sacrifice, and the wood, and the stones, and the dust, and licked up the water that was in the trench" (PhPrv 829; 1 Kings 18:36–38).

171 Jesus answered and said unto them, Destroy this temple, and in three days I will raise it up. (PhPrv 830; John 2:19).

172 "Now faith is the substance of things hoped for, the evidence of things not seen" (PhPrv 837; Hebrews 11:1).

173 "I Jesus have sent mine angel to testify unto you these things in the churches. I am the root and the offspring of David, and the bright and morning star" (PhPrv 840; Revelation 22:16).

174 "The thief cometh not, but for to steal, and to kill, and to destroy: I am come that they might have life, and that they might have it more abundantly" (PhPrv 846; John 10:10).

175 St. Louis Rams and the Tennessee Titans, Super Bowl 34. "4th and Inches," January 30, 2000 (PhPrv 858).

176 "Though I speak with the tongues of men and of angels, and have not charity, I am become as sounding brass, or a tinkling cymbal" (PhPrv 877; 1 Corinthians 13:1).

177 "But if ye had known what this meaneth, I will have mercy, and not sacrifice, ye would not have condemned the guiltless" (PhPrv 883; Matthew 12:7).

178 "Now faith is the substance of things hoped for, the evidence of things not seen" (PhPrv 922; Hebrews 11:1).

179 This poem is a tribute to a man who lived to be 101 years of age. A prophet of God, Reverend Mack Kearse instructed me for nine years in the gospel. Under his tutelage, I witnessed many wonderful acts of God and found for myself the God of legend to be a God of very present reality. At 101 years of age, this man did not look a day over sixty and was the physical equal of a much younger man. According to Acts 2:1–4 the Spirit (and power) of God was at rest continually upon him, which explained his inexplicable youth, vitality and extraordinary works. In June of 1987, at God's appointed time, he was taken on to his heavenly reward. His departure was without long illness or suffering. In the recorded lines of verse lay my tribute to the man whose path crossed mine and whose influence brought me to the place in life I am today.

180 "The way of an eagle in the air; the way of a serpent upon a rock; the way of a ship in the midst of the sea; and the way of a man with a maid" ("If"; Proverbs 30:19).

About the Author

In the 1980's the author's poetry was repeatedly featured in a major Philadelphia newspaper's "Poetry Corner". Several short articles of his, dealing with various political issues of the time were also featured there. In 1989 four of his poems were included in the "American Poetry Anthology" volume IX, Number 4, published by Robert Nelson. In the mid 2000's back-to-back editions of "The International Who's Who In Poetry", Howard Ely Editor, featured two of the author's works. Out of the two-hundred poetry selections appearing in each of the editions, both of the author's poems, one appearing the one year and the other the next, were chosen to be the first poem featured on page number one in each edition.

Born in Philadelphia Pennsylvania and raised by christian grandparents, as a small child the author was very curious-minded. Heavily influenced by his christian up-bringing the author often delved, even at a young age, into his grandfather's small library of books on christian subject matter. He often sat before his grandfather, the pastor of a small church, absorbing the many sermons and subject matter poured out from his grandfather's pulpit. After completing high school, he attended college, but after a few years quit abruptly. There was a deep-seated hunger for the answer to questions on religion and God that had plagued him all his life. At this stage in his life he was convinced of two things: That there was a God who controlled all things, and that there was a path to God accessible to all men. He believed that if a man would sincerely seek he would find a performance of the miraculous works Jesus promised with his words, "… the works that I do, shall he do also; …" John 14:12 kjv. *Philadelphia Proverbs* is a summation of the author's search for the God he always knew to be real.

CPSIA information can be obtained
at www.ICGtesting.com
Printed in the USA
BVHW050516270922
647884BV00001B/4

9 781512 741650